My Mother's Baby

Memoir: Multiple Marriages and Divorces

Shoeshe Berstein

A Spiritual Journey Through Feminism & Online Dating

Contents

Dedication

This book is dedicated to the memory of my younger brother, Steven Vann-Berstein. His passion for music, his devotion to his wife of 34 years, and his love and care for the children they adopted from Russia helped inspire me to pursue my dreams, find my passion and write a book.

Disclaimer

This is a true story about my life. I have not disguised anyone's name. I ask forgiveness if I have offended or hurt someone or their memories of those no longer with us. It was unintentional. I thank God for the family and friends he has given me.

Acknowledgements

I wish to thank all my friends and family who have listened to me talk about writing a book. I am extremely indebted to the following people who encouraged and challenged me to stop talking and start writing.

- The first two people, Norma Baas and Judy Schlief, who read the initial rough draft and made positive comments on my analogies.
- A trusted friend of a friend but a stranger to me, Debbie Porter, who read it with a nonjudgmental critical approach and helped me unscramble my words.
- Still a friend from the third decade of my life, Margaret Montreuil, a trusted believer and published author who likes reading the honest truth.
- An author, friend and future relative to my daughter, Eileen Biernat, who helped me define my focus and purpose for the book and give me a glimpse into the publishing world.
- Without clowning around, my sister-friend, Cathy Taylor, who seriously proofread my earliest manuscript and put loving notations all over it in red ink.
- My Italian-Jewish older sister, Francesca Welsh, who after reading a final draft humbled me with questions like "What would your mother say?"
- A kindred spirit from the first time we met four years ago, Teri Hyrkas, lifted me up with her prayers and writing expertise.

Chapter 1: Letter To Jane

"If you can't tell people what you are doing (or what you have done), maybe you should not be doing it (or not have done it)." —Mother

September 24, 2017

Dear Jane,

I came across your book, *A Round-Heeled Woman: My Late-Life Adventures in Sex and Romance,* during the summer searching the self-help section of the library for a lift. Usually, I buy a pair of shoes or a bra to perk myself up, but this day I was reaching higher. I came across a large, colorful book about prostitution by Gene Simmons—the presence of which in my house upset my husband —and another book, *"Living the Second Half of Your Life on Purpose,"* which brought me hope.

My mother was barely 17 when she had me in 1950. I'm 67. You are the same age my mother would be if she had not died in 2008. Because of her quest for love (and sex), I was looking at dating ads in 1993, and that is how I met my third husband.

Perusing Craigslist in 2010, I didn't expect to meet my fourth husband, who made me his fourth wife. I'm still married to him. I am finally over my first husband, have three grown children with my second, and am still haunted by nightmares of my third.

I want to write a book like yours. At times, I felt you were me, writing under a pen name. I was an English teacher, graduating in 1997, when my children and stepchildren were struggling with "teenhood." I've been journaling regularly most of my life. A plastic tub of journals attesting to my capsulated life remains in the basement. My adventures have been from coast to coast. My multiple marriages and divorces, careers and hobbies, and teaching students in the public, private, and paroled environments account for more successes than failures.

My children aren't married. I'm not a grandmother. I'm like a chameleon, blending in when I can. I hunt, fish, shoot trap, and shoot pool to be my husband's buddy. We met when we were both approaching 60, retired together, and spend most of our time together. I hope that this time we have partners until death do we part. We have good sex, and I've wondered if we are abnormal for our age. I want to write about how good it is to be this age, enjoying retirement with someone with whom I really like having lots of sex. I have overcome stigmas, aliases, and identity crises and am now content to grow old gracefully. There is wisdom here to pass on.

I can't squelch any longer this overwhelming, burning brain sprain to actualize spiritual freedom by writing. As I continue to procrastinate, my bucket list grows. The free piano I acquired helps stretch my brain; a fitness director down the street lets me work out my body three times a week; and my spirit continues to thrive from a wellspring of prayer and Bible study. Since I've espoused, preached, and warned about the threefold aspects of our human struggle to thrive—mental, physical, and spiritual—I'm keenly aware of tapping into my potential on all three before it's too late.

I wonder, can you, would you help me get over myself and out of myself so I write the damn book? If not, if anything, just to tickle you, you might find it amusing that I've also been a professional clown for 10 years, and that doesn't pay crap either.

Sincerely,

Seeking Susan (aka Sally Star Susan Mae Vann-Berstein Stanfa Gross Peacock Tanner Vann-Berstein Hadac—another story about how a woman has to change her name to keep her own identity and survive definition by paperwork.)

One Year Later

R eading Jane's book moved me to action. There were so many connections, "soul ties," a phenomenon that links the reader to the writer like names on a family tree. It seemed as though she was my mother and I in different time zones and in both places at once. Mother-like-daughter, daughter-like-mother, we were connected. I wanted her to know how profoundly grateful I was to find her. I wanted to adopt her.

One month after reading Jane's book, *A Round-Heeled Woman*, I wrote her a letter. A month later, I tried to figure out where to send it. My heart sank when I found her obituary online while searching for an address. The pounding message in my soul was that I had procrastinated once too often. Was I serious about compiling words about myself, about anyone or anything, in one bound volume? Have I been kidding myself all these years about being a writer? Just because I was born on the fifth of July and my mother called me a delayed firecracker doesn't mean I'm necessarily slow or a dud. I've procrastinated long enough. Hindsight is like the warning words on a car's rearview mirrors: Objects in mirror are closer than they appear. Looking back, I don't see how I could have dreamed of writing a book before now. My dreams appeared distant and out of focus, but they didn't pass by me without notice.

"What's your book about?" people ask me. "I'm not sure," I say, groping for a more thought-out answer. "I'm trying to make sense of all the journals I've kept for the last 40 years." I find myself thinking about the book so much that I have to answer the "What are you up to these days?" question with the obsessive truth. "Oh? You're writing a book? Really? What's it about?"

"Well, um, uh, that's my problem. I'm not sure." I couldn't just come out and say it was about sex and relationships. I wondered if it were more about religion and spirituality. Then the idea of wholeness - health and fitness, addictions and recovery crossed my mind and I realized I would not know what the book was about until I wrote it. I could write about my childhood and the parenting skills that I did or did not possess to be a parent. But at this point in the writing process, I am sure that I'm "pot committed," as they say in Poker. I've told so many people that I'm going to write a book that I'm determined. There is no turning back – I have to get it done.

I've contemplated writing a book for as long as I can remember. When I was a little girl, I'd tell myself stories while drifting off to sleep. I'd set the scene, define the characters, and let the script emerge. As time went by and life happened, I thought it would be useless to try to write something fresh and innovative that wasn't already on a bookshelf. I spent many hours reading and decided that my life wasn't so spectacular that the great novel would simply explode from my brain. Nor do I now expect that some of my experiences won't be recognized as similar to the very ones of your mother, your aunt, or your 11th grade English teacher. Even though I have an English degree, the accolades that come with being published aren't the point. The point is that I've lived a life worth writing about. I didn't plan my life like one does a novel with an outline. My memories spilled out like bits and pieces of an old movie showing how life happens with or without a five-year plan.

Jane's book inspired me to come out of the shadows that I'd been hiding behind. The boldness she embodied in her pursuit of what she wanted, where she was in her life, and her decisive plan to get what she wanted was familiar.

Several times in my life, I've made some bold, uncharacteristic decisions that I didn't have the nerve to announce. I've journaled most of them, revisited those writings often, and sometimes remember but don't recognize if that person was really me. I've surprised myself more looking back at where I've come from to determine how I got here. What I thought was a hard, painful event then now seems like a joyful memory of an accomplishment. By the grace of God, the past I've written about wasn't as bad as I thought. I made it sound worse with the words I chose. My life embarrassed me. I was ashamed of my family's history of broken relationships and divorces. And I certainly didn't want people to know I had been married before I was married to the father of my children. The stigma of being married and divorced once isn't so bad. But the second time, dealing with the children and the church, I felt like I was swimming upstream.

I wasn't going back, but I was going in an unexpected direction. It even seemed less stigmatizing to know some people had multiple intimate relationships. If they had several sexual partners, they didn't have to change their name or address. They probably didn't tell their mother or their employer about their affair. Women more often feel pressured to be secretive about their different relationships. Men don't experience the same problems or suffer the negative judgments of dealing with multiple marriages and divorces. Some men even brag about their one-night stands or extramarital affairs. The playing field isn't level, and there are no written rules for this adventure and their advantage.

Throughout this journey, I studied the Bible and self-help books in order to survive the struggles of loneliness and shame without the support of an extended family. Friends came and went, just as the relatives of my past did. I either moved away and lost contact or they passed away. The only consistent part of me was my relationship with God. Through everything, I've decided I am the biggest hypocrite I know. As much as I seek the Lord, I'd expect to behave differently and have walked a more righteous path.

And God said,
"I will always love you and
I will never leave you."

I've said in my heart that God was/is the most important being in my life and in my death. He is the constant, consistent comforter of my soul in this life and the next. People will come and go, and some will make us happy for a short time or a long time. Some will disappoint us and break promises. But God is always there and never leaves us. He is the only truth holding up the definitions of "always" and "never." If I truly believe this, then my story, my life, has a purpose, a point that I'm not fully aware of and am only now, finally, trusting to share with others.

Shocked is how I would describe my initial response to the beginning of Jane's book. I realized that she was bold and courageous for her age at a time before online dating was normal. What some viewed as unsavory behavior for a woman of her means is now accepted as commonplace. Similarly, I could not, before now, have written the accounts you're about to read. Jane's experiences touched my spirit and something ignited within me.

Chapter 2: Practice Makes Perfect

At first I thought my book would be about my three marriages. I wanted to believe that my third husband was my muse and that I was in a position to write for a purpose. The purpose, the point, was that God is in control. He's in charge of our lives, regardless of—or, more pointedly, in spite of—what we choose. But then, when my third husband and I divorced, I felt like Oblio in the Pointless Forest. If you don't know the story, The Point is the name of a Harry Nilsson record album in the 1970s about a boy named Oblio who has a round head in a world of people with pointed heads. He wears a pointed cap to hide his pointless head but is eventually banished from the land of Point, with his dog Arrow, to the Pointless Forest. He goes through the forest, learning with every fork in the road that everything in the forest does indeed have a point. When he ends up back in the land of Point, all the townspeople are surprised to see him and discover that, under his cap, Oblio does, in fact, have a point. And thus, my story starts out like a fairytale with no point.

Goldilocks and her three husbands sounded like a relevant title for my book. Inquiring minds need to know how a nice Baptist girl from New Jersey, born blonde and determined not to act like a ditz, bimbo, or stupid girl, wound up in Minnesota, married multiple times. How does a first-born overachiever, educated to be a career woman, steered to play the game of life in a man's world, determined not to let money and power corrupt her, manage to get sucked into the backlash of 1970s feminism? Feeling deceived, tricked, and man-ipulated, I simply didn't understand why I felt set up and used. I didn't blame God. I wasn't angry with Him. I didn't believe He created me to just shut up and look pretty. But I wasn't hitting the mark. I didn't know what I was aiming for. What was the point of my life?

My mother sent me a poster once that said, "God doesn't make mistakes." He created me as an independent, talented woman. My responsibility to discover all that encompassed would depend on my choices. The trouble with me was that I didn't know what I wanted and I didn't want to disappoint my mother. I bought the propaganda that I could be anything I wanted to be if I set my mind to it. God also created my past, my lineage, and my roots, all of which would determine my future. I wanted to have a large family, but that wasn't part of God's plan. I couldn't see any satisfactory future in having a job for the sole purpose of making money.

The dream of designing and sewing clothing didn't seem realistic. I gave up the fantasy of being a singer or a dancer when I was 9 years old. A woman from the baby boomer generation, I had a chance to climb the corporate ladder and become a woman of means. The encouragement I received determined my choice between what I truly wanted to be and what I thought others wanted me to be. In order to please and not disappoint, I let others choose for me. Several years as a secretary honed my writing skills, and the money was good, but I was not writing what I wanted to write. I can see my mistakes now, and I'm still learning from them. Returning to our first love, our childhood joys and dreams, brings us right back to where we left off, only to discover what we couldn't put off any longer.

The last 5 months of my younger brother's life, I decided to stop procrastinating on the piano lessons I dreamed about as a kid. My brother was a gifted musician, wasting away with cancer, and he was overjoyed when I acquired a free piano and started where my lessons as a child ended, teaching myself from beginner lesson books. As fate would have it, this was also the year Jane Juska died before I mailed her the letter I wrote after reading her book. I told Steven about the book and how it reminded me of our mother and her search for dance partners through dating ads in the 1990s.

Telling him the whole story made my skin prickle with goose bumps. My "aha moment" was that my procrastinating had led to missed opportunities. I told Steven that day that I would write the book I'd dreamed about since I was a kid.

"That's great. That's really great. Good for you. You should do it."

After he swallowed, gulped, and took a labored breath, he added, "What's it about?"

Half reluctant to get too deep, I replied, "I don't know exactly, but you're in it. We're having a conversation out on the deck, and you're smoking a cigar."

He was likely wishing he could have one at that moment and said, "Wow, that's something. But maybe you should leave this chapter out."

"That's funny," I said. "Mother used to say that all the time." If you asked a question she didn't want to answer or asked too many questions, she'd say, "Are you writing a book?" My puzzled response was, "No! Why? What do you mean?

"Leave this chapter out," she'd say, which sounded like a rebuke coming from her. Mother could be rather sarcastic sometimes, and cynical. She could turn just about anything into suspicious contempt of human nature, doubting one's motives. Too bad she was often so distrusting, negative, and fearful.

We didn't discuss it, but my brother knew he was a lot like our mother. And now I wonder if he really thought I should leave out the chapter with him in it or if he was just being sarcastic like Mom. Is it in our DNA that we act like our parents? Are our choices truly our choices? Another title for my book, Soul Ties, tries to reconcile the parents to the children and the children to their parents, and their choices as a result of their parents' influence. Do we repeat the "sins of the father" because it's in our DNA? Do we repeat patterns and mistakes because they're familiar, comfortable, and somewhat predictable?

Steven, like Mother, spent many days just sitting, smoking, and staring out the window. Other days he lived and breathed to write songs and play music. Like our father, he dreamed of making it big in the music industry. Why didn't my brother ever try to get his music published or recorded?

My brother would have been 65 this May. I envied his musical abilities and admired his dedication. I wondered why I wasn't born with a passion for something the way Steven enjoyed music. He probably had perfect pitch. He started playing the drums at 5 years old. In his teens, while recovering from rheumatic fever in a children's hospital and missing a year of school, he learned to play the guitar. By 19, he had taught himself how to play the piano. He wrote and recorded music, playing several instruments and singing in four-part harmony, layering track on track. He'd record one part with one instrument and then layer on top another track, another instrument, and another harmony, four tracks in all. Yeah, yeah, yeah. The Beatles were already doing this, but there were four of them. Steven was one man "Berstein at the seams," dedicated to the music he loved.

Steven was able to break our family record for short-term marriages. He was married once, until death-do part. He met his wife Vicki while he was performing in a nightclub. She was a college student letting her hair down one of the few times before graduating into the corporate world. They were married for 35 years and lived in 8 states. Steven and Vicki traveled up in the world and around in the country as Vicki's career advanced. As child-rearing years slipped by them, retirement loomed on the horizon. They began to wonder about their legacy as midlife approached. At 50 years old, Steven and Vicki adopted an infant son from Russia naming him Steven. Two years latter they adopted a baby girl from the same orphanage and named her Vikki. My brother Steven held the family together as a stay-home parent. He was like a mother hen, keeping the kids on schedules and encouraging his wife to bring home the bacon. Steven was Vicki's rock. He was the anchor that kept her from drifting off course, or giving up in a male dominated corporate business world. He is still a beacon of light shining the way home for his children. From Russia, or France, from East coast to West, Steven's love for his family lives through his history. Maybe if the children read this memoir they will get a glimpse of where their adoptive parents came from and how blessed they are to be part of this family.

Chapter 3: Jewish Roots (Paternal Grandparents And Urban Renewal)

R emember what you learned in kindergarten? If you can, was it everything you needed to know to survive childhood, your teen years, adolescence, and early adulthood and be accountable? Remember how you could hardly wait for your birthday and the first day of each new school year? The years you were finally old enough to drive, drink, or vote were milestones. The age to get married and have kids was obscure. Some turning points in life required tests; others—maybe ones that were more important and should have—did not. Somewhere between your first and 31st birthdays, you could celebrate your golden year, a special year when your age matched the calendar day you were born.

On my golden birthday, I turned 5 years old. I was staying with my grandparents on my father's side. My father's sister, Aunt Jackie, was having her first child, and my mother and 2-year-old brother, Steven, went to Philadelphia, where Jackie lived, to help her with her new baby. Sandy, my cousin, was born on July 5, my golden birthday.

Staying with my grandparents could have been fun if I didn't dwell on the darkness of their tiny apartment. They lived across the street from the elementary school in three rooms behind their storefront dressmaking shop, where customers came to see Grand-Mère (the name we called my grandmother), Marcelle Berstein. She was born in La Rochelle, France, a seaside resort similar to Atlantic City. Whether she was afraid of being deported or lost isn't clear, but she always wore a secret pocket around her waist with her "papers." Men's hats and women's bonnets were part of her trade back home. The Easter parades on the boardwalk in Atlantic City were spectacular in the 1920s and '30s and brought back memories of the good old days in her native land. She took photographs to capture those memories, mostly in black and white, which are forgotten somewhere, in someone's closet.

My grandmother was full of creative energy. She was barely 4'11", wore size 5 shoes, and had tiny hands. She produced exquisite, intricate sewing designs with expensive fabrics. My grandmother prattled with a thick, French accent, welcoming patrons to her shop. When she came to America, she didn't speak any English. Raising two babies in a foreign country without family during the '20s must have been an exciting, tumultuous time. It might have driven me to drink, but she seemed self- controlled and stoic. She claimed no particular religion, saying she was a free thinker.

An entertainer at heart, she made costumes for herself and others. After my grandfather died, Madame Marcelle visited the nursing homes in her neighborhood. The patrons looked forward to my grandmother dressing up as a gypsy for Halloween, a bunny for Easter, and Mrs. Claus at Christmas. She would play the piano for them and lead them in song. She'd make them laugh and on occasion, didn't understand when they were laughing at her. In her French slur of H and R, she could envision why a person would call her a character or a pistol, but why a hot rod? She never learned how to drive a car or ride a bicycle.

I was in the third grade when I wanted to learn how to speak French so my mother allowed me to walk three blocks to Grand-Mère's apartment for a French lesson. I'd have to cross over Atlantic Avenue watching out for city buses or Jitneys (a 10 passenger van that traveled primarily on Pacific Avenue). Busy streets with heavy traffic were never a problem when I was growing up. As I got older there was a greater concern for deserted streets, especially after dark. I'd arrive at Grand-Mère's apartment on time and ready for my French lesson. She continued to do sewing alterations and dress making from her apartment and occasionally had a customer when I arrived. "Oh la la, mon petit cochon," she'd say to me. It was a term of endearment, as she looked me up and down as if to size me up and go over my attire. Then she'd introduced me to her patron as her oldest granddaughter but I knew she was calling me her little piggy.

Grand-Mère continued to make her way into the spotlights during Atlantic City's rebirth of the 1970's. In August of 1977 the Atlantic County Federation of Senior Citizen Clubs held the first Ms. Senior Citizen Pageant. At 78 years old Marcelle (Frenchy) Berstein received a 3 foot trophy, a crown and a trip to Hawaii for her "Inner Beauty." Atlantic City grew crowded and corrupt with casinos during the 1980's and Grand-Mère was forced to retire to Florida after a motorcycle accident. Her last years were spent in a wheel chair. "Oh la la, ki la hora," she'd say when she was upset telling her story. I always thought she was swearing in French until years later I heard a Yiddish word, kina hora, and began to wonder about Grand-Mère's Jewish roots. She was not driving or riding the day of the accident. A careless driver hit her, a pedestrian, who walked everywhere. Her daily walks to and from the boardwalk ended and she died in Ocala, Florida, miles from the seashore she loved.

My grandfather Jack was a WWI and WWII veteran, and God only knows what his pain was like. I always remember him as being in a bathrobe, rather grouchy. He grumped at me about sucking my thumb and threatened to put his nasty, stinky medicine on it so I wouldn't want to put it in my mouth. He was born in Lithuania during the early 1900s. Persecution drove his Jewish family out, and eventually, they came to America. He met my grandmother in France, where he was a serviceman in the US Army while procuring hats for the soldiers. My grandfather's family, the Bersteins, didn't have much to do with him after his marriage to my grandmother. Jack's parents were observant Jews from Vineland, New Jersey. My dad said his father was considered the black sheep of the family. Was my grandfather ostracized for marrying a shiksa (a non- Jewish woman)? Years later I would learn more about the persecution of the Jews around the world and wonder if, in fact, my Grand-Mère was a French Jew and afraid of being identified as such. My dad never went to synagogue; his sister did, but I don't believe she had a bat mitzvah even though she was born around 1922 when girls were included in the ceremony.

My father was named after the French general Joffre, but he may have had a Napoleon complex. His physical growth appeared stunted, possibly by poor health or merely genetics. By the age of 12, he'd suffered bad eyesight and polio. Thanks to Grand-Mère's homeopathic attention to Dad's legs and feet, he was able to recover from the polio and walk again. He didn't complete eighth grade, and his dreams of flying airplanes or playing big-band music never materialized. Dad watched his father's health decline as a result of being a wounded veteran, complicated by drugs and alcohol. Most of my dad's childhood passed in the shadows of sickness, drugs, alcohol, and illicit sex.

His father and his older sister, Jackie, were unknown entertainers in Atlantic City. Jackie was a singer. I never got to hear her sing, but she was beautiful, with striking, coal black hair and dark blue eyes. Grandpop (Smiling Jack Vann) had a reputation in the Vaudeville circuit as something of a song and dance man. Grand-Mère's career mushroomed into a well-known seamstress of designer dresses and costumes for stage performance. Jack drove cabs, created playbills, and quite possibly sold whatever the nightlife crowds wanted in order to get protection from the mob: recreational drugs, marijuana, alcohol.

My father followed in his father's corrupt footsteps. The fact that he could walk and even dance was part of his charm. In spite of his educational setbacks and shady financial setups, my father acted like an entertainer without actually trying. His polished looks and occasional French comments attracted attention. Dad was an extremely handsome young man and an impeccably dressed bachelor when he met my mother at the Steel Pier in the late 1940s. Once a popular place, with many piers for entertainment and new talent performing daily, Atlantic City's resort reputation was scarred by wars and storms. The famous Steel Pier at the end of Virginia Avenue boasted about the entertainment of a high diving horse, an ocean bottom diving bell and musical dancing waters. Talent scouts continued to hold events looking for new talent, but the searches declined throughout the years before I was born.

There were live bands and a variety of famous musicians every week in the summer. A children's theater featured young singers and dancers from New York, Philadelphia, New Jersey, and other eastern states that I didn't know existed when I was young. In our close, compact neighborhoods, it wasn't uncommon to hear the music of a piano or violin coming from a nearby house. I once heard a grammar-school acquaintance singing "Bye Bye Blackbird" and thought she sounded professional. My Aunt Jackie (her stage name was Jacqueline Deauville when she appeared at the Savoy Club in Montreal, Canada), sang professionally when she was a young woman. She performed in nightclubs around Atlantic City when the Miss America Pageant was still a famous seashore attraction. Jackie didn't make it big, but she got the fame and attention that my father longed for as a young man.

Joffre Vann-Berstein never realized his dream of being a musician in the big- band era of Gene Krupa and Jimmy Dorsey. Naturally, he was proud of his son, who began imitating Davy Crockett, a cowboy hero, at 2 years old and Ricky Nelson when he was 4. My brother Steven had visions of playing drums onstage in front of live audiences one day. I remember Dad setting up a full drum set in the tiny living room of our two-story apartment on Massachusetts Avenue. Those few family performances brought us all together, with Dad and Steven drumming while Mommy and I danced.

Dad and Steven each had a seat in front of the drums. Several sets of drumsticks, wire brushes, tom-toms, and cymbals crackled and crashed like thunder out our windows. I never gave it a thought before, but what must the neighbors have been saying? Did anyone enjoy the "music" coming from our third-floor flat?

Did anyone question whether it was live music or a Gene Krupa record turned up to full volume? Were we all just having fun, or was there some hope that we would be heard and discovered by a passing talent scout?

When we were young, I envied my brother's talent and the attention he got from our father. My dad would have liked to play music professionally, so living vicariously through his son triggered emotions. Steven made a name for himself in local bands around the Jersey shore area in the 1970s and '80s. Dad would show up at Steven's gigs intoxicated and brag about his son.

I wasn't in New Jersey when Steven dealt with this embarrassment and eventually tried to help Dad get treatment. All I could do was pray and thank God that I wasn't in Atlantic City. That whole scene scared me.

Rich people drifted in and out of Atlantic City from Hollywood, Las Vegas, Chicago, and New York. Politics, prostitutes, gambling, guns, and gangs stormed in eroding the delicate, sandy shoreline. As tides go in and out, so do entrepreneurs looking for ways to capitalize on what keeps an island resort with so many wandering souls afloat. All those visitors needed places to stay and transportation to shows and restaurants for breakfast, lunch, and dinner. Some needed protection, connections, drugs, and other diversions. My dad, being Jack Berstein's son, was a jack-of-all-trades like his father. With only an eighth-grade education, a small handgun under his belt, and his sharp looks, short stature, and sweet talk, Dad wedged himself into the nooks and crannies of numerous small jobs.

Like his father, my dad did what he could to make money by meeting the needs of people around him. At some point in their careers, they drove taxicabs and limousines. Dad managed garages, but I never saw him with dirty hands, so he couldn't have been a mechanic. Back in the '50s and '60s, a garage was more of a facility to park cars. Wealthy people would drive in from out of state, park their cars for days, weeks, or the entire summer, and hire people to get them around the island. Between music gigs in the '70s and '80s, my brother chauffeured limousines from airports to hotels and casinos during Atlantic City's rebirth and growth into a gambling competitor to Las Vegas.

Talent and pageantry came and went constantly in Atlantic City, as did famous actors, musicians, and singers, who lit up the nightlife of the beach resort. Money flowed like wine while the ocean waves melodically rolled in and out with the tides. Unlike the desert of Las Vegas, Atlantic City, a suburb of Absecon Island, sits next to the ocean.

Most people called it a vacation resort town, but not the locals, those who lived there all year round.

Atlantic City had two bridge roads out to the mainland, and one other suburb on the southern end of the island had its own bridge to higher ground. The Miss America Pageant, which was born there in 1921, helped grow the city in the '20s and '30s to be a hot entertainment spot on the Jersey coast. Hoping to lift spirits up from the Great Depression, a man from Philadelphia invented the game Monopoly. My story takes root on the streets named on the Monopoly board and sandy beaches at which those streets dead-ended.

The boardwalk stretched 6 miles along the shoreline, from the inlet where I grew up to the suburb on the other end of the island, called Longport. When gambling became legal and the casinos changed the skyline of Atlantic City, a full generation of islanders was either displaced or changed careers. Urban renewal was long overdue, and the youth of the 1970s were moving on, moving out, or going along with the born- again experience of a new generation. Buying and selling properties and moving millions of dollars up and down the boardwalk and city streets of Absecon Island was not merely a board game anymore.

Chapter 4: Christian Roots (Maternal Grandparents, Rock & Roll, Cars, & Sex)

S aturday nights in the 1940s and '50s brought crowds of young people to the boardwalk piers and lounges to see and hear big bands play. Dance floors never seemed big enough back then. It was one of those nights when Doris met Joffre. My mother—her given name was Doris, but Dad always called her Dottie—was 16. My father, Joffre, was 22. Mother was Baptist. Dad was Jewish. My grandmother Rose, Mommy's mom, was not happy. Whether she was distressed over her young daughter dating an older guy or just fed up with the closed-in feeling of the city "going to hell in a hand basket," as she'd say, Rose decided to take my mother on a train to California.

I'm not sure why Mother and Mom Mom had gone to California without her husband, Charles (Bus), the year my uncle was conceived. My grandparents were either living apart or living together in disharmony. Rose loved Bus, her husband of 16 years, but they both had baggage that split them apart and set them on separate, sad paths.

Rose was one of five children and a descendant of three fading decades of Pennsylvania Dutch religiosity. She took up the chores of motherhood for her siblings after her mother passed from pneumonia. Rose struggled and stressed as a teenager through war and the Depression. WWI and WWII would have been consuming circumstances of her life, as more women were put to work in the predominantly male workforce. The roaring '20s, Prohibition, gambling, and a sexual revolution on the horizon shaped Rose's world. Decadent lifestyles, inebriated choices, and illegal profits and losses surrounded and drowned Rose's godly virtues, passed down from her mother, shattering family continuity. To make matters worse, Rose's older sister, Dorothy, didn't know how to keep her legs together. Every year she had another baby, another burden, as if the family weren't overloaded enough. Rose and Dorothy's father, my widowed great-grandfather, had a difficult time feeding all those children. He finally called the Board of Health and Welfare to remove Dorothy's children from his home, putting her seven offspring in foster care.

My grandmother's young life without a mother was not her choice. She had to make the best of it. Setting boundaries lifted some burden off my grandmother's back so she could start to enjoy her life, ride around in cars, go to military dances, and experience movie houses. All of this background weaves like a thread into my conception.

How grandmother Rose met my grandfather Charles "Bus" Britton Adams is a mystery to me. It is one of those pieces of information I never heard or thought to ask about. But deductive reasoning puts their meeting between WWI and WWII, before Bus went overseas with the army. Rose got pregnant before they were married. I can't imagine my grandmother not knowing how that happened. There's no excuse in light of the fact that her mother left this earth fairly young after having a few babies herself. But it begs the question, before birth control pills and legal abortions, how did young women learn about sex? How did they learn about love, lovemaking, and making babies? How did they learn about making a home and a family where a man and a woman become husband and wife until death do they part? Are the carmakers responsible for the beginning of the sexual revolution, the rock and roll in the backseat that's blamed for the start of the baby boom of the 1950s and '60s? How does all this background shape my being?

Rose and Bus got married. They had to. Did Rose's father insist? Did Rose carry on about "What if something happens to Bus in the war' because then the baby would be fatherless and nameless? Or was it shame and humiliation because Rose knew better? It doesn't really matter now, except to note that Rose had a miscarriage after they were married. My mother told me this story, and I remember her clearly saying, "That baby died." My grandmother's marriage certificate was among her personal papers when she died. It showed she had lied about the date she was married, probably to figure in 9 months for the baby. Rose's mother's marriage certificate was also found with the treasured memorabilia. It was clearly altered to show the date of marriage earlier than their oldest child, Dorothy's, birthday, meaning Rose's mother, in spite of her religious, Pennsylvania Dutch background, had to get married because she was pregnant, and Rose repeated history. The point is, Rose and Bus got married because of that baby. My mother was conceived from that union and born in 1933.

No doubt my grandmother Rose was a strong, independent young woman with determination. Her childhood was shortened by early responsibilities for her father and siblings. She was a good-looking woman of about 5'6" with brown eyes, a cherry-shaped nose, and a dark complexion with freckles and later, lots of wrinkles. Before going to California, Rose and her daughter Doris had been moving around from apartment to apartment. Rose worked in a sewing factory. Bus minimally contributed to their living arrangements. He liked to fish, but I don't know if he ever did any professional commercial fishing. He spent most of his time in bars "drinking and God knows what else," Rose would say with a forced laugh. Mother said there were many nights when Bus did not come home, and when he did make it, often he'd have been in a fight. There were fights at home too. Furniture was flying, and there were fewer groceries as time went on. I'm still trying to find out what Bus did in the army and how messed up he might have been, coming back from the war. My memories of him are as a gentle, soft-spoken man with a square jaw. He was very tall man, with long legs and light blue eyes. He lived with Hilda, his common-law wife, who was short and round.

At Christmas when I was growing up, Pop Pop and Hilda would visit us and bring presents. Hours after they left, Mom Mom and Joby (I assume her common-law husband) would stop by with more presents. I don't know how old I was when I learned that Mom Mom and Pop Pop were married and were my mother's parents. I don't know when I decided that it was important to know why they didn't live together. All I knew was that they separated sometime before my mother was 16, when she and her mother went to California. Years later I heard about Mom Mom meeting someone named Finis (not sure if this is his first or last name) in California the summer they crossed the country in a train. Uncle Charlie, my mother's half-brother, tried to find Finis after his mother died, and the truth came out about Charlie's real father. As things have a way of turning out, Charlie lived in California while in the navy, from 1967 to 1971. He married and settled in Santa Barbara.

Twenty years later, after Rose died, he discovered his father wasn't who he thought was his father and that his biological father lived and died in Santa Barbara.

Chapter 5: Broken Families Were My Role Models

From East Coast to West Coast and somewhere in the middle, wherever we start, that's where we wind up in the end. Scripture says that the day of one's death is better than the day of one's birth. And it doesn't end when we die. It's circular. There is nothing new under the sun. We came from ashes, we return to ashes. I want my ashes scattered in the Atlantic Ocean off Atlantic City. The beginning of the story, the beginning of my story, the beginning of your story, started before you were born. My story began on the East Coast, or did it? I left home at 17 for the West Coast. I wound up in the middle of the country, the Midwest. Even though some things look the same but are different, they reflect repeated events or the memories of them. Does history repeat itself, or do we just do the same familiar things over and over again until we change? Groundhog Day is somewhat real for some of us. Some of our families' stories blur the lines between images of our very existence and our ancestors'.

My mother's big adventure to California took place in 1948. My grandmother's baby, Charlie, my mother's half-brother, was born in September 1949 in Atlantic City, New Jersey. Rose named him Charles Britton Adams II, after her estranged husband. Mother eloped with Joffre, my father, shortly thereafter. They had to go to Maryland, because my mother was underage and lied about her birthday to get the marriage license. It appears that she didn't have to get married. No doubt having heard her mother's horror stories of taking care of her baby brothers and sister, Doris was going to escape before she became attached to her mother's baby. Any 16-year-old girl who was unhappy at home would look elsewhere for love, comfort, and fun. She had an unstable home life. Her father was a war veteran and an alcoholic and her mother was in charge. Little did my mother realize the affect environmental influences of her parents would have on her life. How did she cope with the knowledge that her brother's father was not her father? Chances are, my mother escaped to pursue her dreams by riding around in cars, smoking and drinking. She had no idea that her father's drinking and her mother's sister's alcoholism would trickle down to her drinking habits.

Mother met Reggie when Rose met Finis in California. It turns out that 60 years later, my mother often wondered what happened to Reggie. It wasn't until after my grandmother died that my mother attempted, in vain, to make contact with her old flame. Was he a lover before my father, before my sister's father? With Reggie in the back of her mind, was my dad the guy on the rebound? Mom had a few other friends that she'd danced with at the Steel Pier in Atlantic City as a teenager. She never expected to see any of them again, nor could she have ever dreamed that one in particular, Gus, would be there for her many years later and become a first-time father to her third child. Fast-forward to 1970, when my mother met Gus through a friend at work. Mother remembered him as a great dancer back in 1948. They practically picked up where they left off 22 years earlier, got married, decided to remodel the kitchen, and instead had a child together. Some heavenly dances are just too divine for a teenager to believe dreams can come true.

Identity Crisis: I Can Do It Myself

My mother was barely 17 when I was born in 1950. Her birthday was June 28. She called me a delayed firecracker because I waited until 10:00 AM on July 5 to make my way into the world. What did she, a teenager, know about parenting? What does anyone know about anything until they experience it first-hand? Mother was 16 when her brother was born. Ten months before I was born. Whether she considered him her real brother is debatable.

Mother's cousin Joanne, one of Aunt Dorothy's children, related memories of how surprised she was to see me as an infant. She thought my mother had a baby doll in the stroller. Thank God, I wasn't mistaken for Mother's puppy, Pudgy, that she dressed in baby clothes when she was younger and pushed around in a baby buggy. Doris, like her mother, enjoyed sewing and making her own outfits, and now mine. I was probably dressed and re-dressed several times a day, for every different occasion, event, or mood, or after every meal. I was my mother's miniature mannequin to design for and dress in clothes she made herself. She was still a teenager, fascinated by Hollywood stars, movies, theaters, and dance. She probably dreamed of fashion and fame. Here I was, her little doll, replacing the puppy in baby clothes, replacing her Hollywood fashion dreams of designing and sewing for the stars. A career for a woman in the 1950s was still a dream.

God doesn't suffer from identity crises, but I do. How I dress and how I think I look provoke me to wonder who I think I am. Somewhere in my childhood, I learned that clothing was important. If one of my grandmothers or my mother handcrafted an article of clothing for me, it was precious, made with tender loving care. They weren't always functional outfits, but they were fashionable and pleasing to the eye. It behooves me some days to know how to dress for the weather and the circumstances of the day. The people I meet and places I visit inspire me to present my best self to perform the tasks at hand. Dressing for the occasion has little to do with looking like you fit the part, as if in a play, and more that you play the part you think you're dressed for. For example, I would no more garden in my Sunday best than go to church in my motorcycle attire. But it isn't the clothing that makes the person any more than a book cover determines the contents of the book.

We are not to judge others. That's God's job. But it is human nature to evaluate and sum up what we see with respect to what we believe. The sight of certain articles of clothing can skew our perception if what we see doesn't line up with our expectations.

Dressing a dog in baby clothes does not make it a baby. Putting girls' clothing on a boy doesn't make him a girl, and vice versa. In days gone by, when girls seldom wore pants and few boys expressed an interest in wearing girls' clothes, neither would confess to cursing God for creating them male or female. "Tomboys" and "sissies" acted out for a while, playing the other side, until they got the message from others that it was not acceptable. They were taught that girls roughhousing like boys and boys going through emotional stages like a girl were normal, but that they would need to put away childish behaviors when they grew up.

For me, when I got hand-me-down jeans and Buster Brown oxford shoes from my Uncle Charlie, I could pretend to be a boy. He was 10 months older than I was, and we were like brother and sister until I was 8 years old. He lived on the mainland, which was like living in the country compared with the city sidewalks, beaches, and boardwalk of Absecon Island. He could dig in the dirt, climb trees, build forts with a hammer and nails, drive tractors, and ride horses. The appeal of country living countered the prissy demands I felt being a girl on the island. I spent my time on beaches, building sandcastles with vacationing kids I'd never met before and would never see again.

Collecting sand crabs and seashells occupied most of my days, sunning and swimming on the Atlantic shore. After a day at the beach and an eyeful of all shapes and sizes of nearly naked bodies, I looked forward to washing off the salt and sand and putting on a cotton T-shirt and a pair of days-of-the-week panties. But I didn't look forward to dressing up if we were going out. When I look back at the photogenic Shirley Temple clone my mother attempted to re-create, the dresses were lovely and the hairdos cute and curly, but I was miserable. A new dress and freshly coiffed hair meant "don't get mussed up." There was no playing in the dirt in a dress. I was not free. There was freedom in the dirt. It goes back to a sixth sense that all life begins and ends in the dirt. Man was formed by God out of clay and returns to the earth, eventually turning to ashes. My new dresses were patterns of grave clothes, lovely, crisp, lively fabrics on the outside covering a prickly, smoldering little body underneath. It was as if the jacket was on the wrong book; the inside title didn't match the outside. Bound up inside were words of joy and sorrow, silenced by a code of restraint that dictated, "children are to be seen and not heard."

The signs we seek that prove God communicates with His children are seen in the symbolism of one's experiences. Proof He knows and cares about us shows up in hindsight like touchstones, rocks crying out. That tongue-tied child whose angelic, Shirley Temple-curled head beamed back at me from the photo pages of my mind was silently screaming to an unknown creator. Wishing I were born a boy didn't seem sinful at the time. Wondering about freedom, getting dirty, yelling, screaming, talking fast and loudly barking orders, which were all things boys engaged in with little restraint, frustrated me and stunted my growth. Or was it part of God's plan that my fuse be longer, so I didn't explode prematurely? There was an unknown part of me that wanted to be heard on the inside. A yearning grew within me to see, hear, and feel a father, a husband, a man who understood the very core—the kishkas—of me. But who could live up to my expectations? I longed for a man to show me what God looked like by loving his wife and children as God loves His children.

After my mother died in 2008, my half sister and I were talking about dates. I needed to double-check the marriage certificate of my mother and father. Was she pregnant with me before she got married? The story I got was how she and my dad eloped one night, driving to Maryland, where they could get married right away. Why? Just to have first-time sex? Mother told me once, during an attempt to talk to me about sex, that my father wouldn't touch her until they got married. I'm not sure if I believed that then, or even now. In fact, I'm less likely to bet on it, knowing what I know now. After all, I am my mother's daughter. At the time of "the talk," it was too late. I'd been sexually active for at least a year. I was 15.

Back then I had no concept of what it was like for my mother to be pregnant with me at 16. I had no contraception to prevent pregnancy when I was 15. Relying on my boyfriend for condoms and to pull out before ejaculation, I was in the same flight pattern as my mother and grandmother. Not until my daughter was 17 did I deeply explore the possibility of her being a mother at such a young age. I flashed back, and my daughter was me: finishing high school, contemplating college, dating a boy whose family life she'd adopted to fill the void of her own divorced family. It clicked. The familiar scenario, the trap that causes young women, including me, to romanticize about love and babies, was a repeating pattern in my family. Is that when the nesting instinct is the strongest? Thinking, I'll build my own nest, my own family to fill my life, to fill me up or pour out my love on? I can understand now what my mother and grandmother feared for me, as I was growing up and riding around in cars with boys.

My own struggle between picking a career after high school and raising a family flooded my brain while fretting over my daughter's choices. Her outstanding school records mirrored my own. I was 34 when she was born, and when she was 17, dating, graduating high school, and contemplating college, I was 51 and having too many flashbacks. I graduated in the top third of 500 students and was the first in two generations to graduate high school. With a strong reading and writing proficiency, many opportunities could have been mine. The easiest choice at the time was to take off to California to be with my future husband. It seemed a logical transition from a broken family, poverty, and a decaying resort island on its way to redevelopment.

Chapter 6: I Write, Therefore I Am

Writing is cathartic for some people, like making music is for others. You keep writing or playing until you make your mark and hit your goal. You write and rewrite until you can see what you hear yourself saying. You continue to create music until you hear the song that has been playing over and over in your head. Whether notes are sentences on paper or the notes on the musical scale, they eventually flow together in a rhythmic movement, touching the deep recesses of your soul. The push, the anticipated sense of satisfaction, comes when others hear you (or that you are heard at all).

I don't know if all I ever needed to know I learned in kindergarten, but I know I resisted conforming to some rules of procedure. It started somewhere, sometime before I knew what was happening. Research points to children's earliest character development as a result of environment and social influences. I remember being as young as 5 years old, grouped in a circle of chairs, waiting for my turn to read. I was not good at waiting. I'd be preoccupied with the prickles in my foot because it fell asleep while sitting on it. I may have had attention deficit before it was a disorder. The teacher, Mrs. Roth, wanted me to repeat kindergarten because I was having difficulty focusing on letters and words in a book. I already knew how to read. I was totally bored with Fun with Dick and Jane. I'd stare out the window, pretending I wasn't there, hoping that they'd all go away.

About that same time, my parents started dropping me off at the Baptist church for Sunday school every week. My grandmother Rose made sure I got my first Bible and let me know she was praying for me. That made me wonder. Why was she praying for me? Was it a good thing or a bad thing?

What did she have to tell God about me? Was there something wrong with me? Did I need prayer for some kind of protection, or did I need a cure for a sickness I didn't know I had? The church became my sanctuary. I loved my Sunday school teachers, the Bible stories, the friends I made there, and, eventually, the Sunday school bus that faithfully arrived on time at 20 South Massachusetts Avenue every Sunday morning. I learned about God and asked Jesus into my heart at that Baptist church on North Carolina and Pacific avenues in Atlantic City. My first Sunday school teachers were Mr. and Mrs. A., but Phoebe Frye encouraged me to write in the front of my Bible the date when I first asked Jesus to come into my heart. I loved God and wanted to be a good Christian.

Reading became a way to escape my life at home. I read every day, every night, everything I could get my hands on, especially the Bible. The summer I turned 9, the elementary school across the street opened its library to the public. We were allowed to check out books with a library card after filling out an application. The librarian wouldn't issue me a card until I could spell out the name of my street instead of abbreviating Massachusetts. She emphasized that, "after all, we were at the Massachusetts Avenue Elementary School." I was upset with that librarian at first but got to like her because of the books she'd suggest. After reading all the horse books for girls and the Hardy Boys mysteries for boys, she introduced me to Daphne du Maurier, even now one of my favorite authors. I don't know if her books were actually appropriate for my age. They seemed provocative, mysterious, and even dark for impressionable young minds. But du Maurier is French, and so am I.

I was French and Jewish, going to a Baptist church, and my

parents didn't go to church at all. It was in fall of that same year that our church group went to a Billy Graham crusade at the YMCA just down the street from the church. I remember getting all fired up at that rally and excited to tell others about Jesus. I rededicated my life to Jesus and wrote the date in the front of my Bible, under the first time I asked Jesus into my heart. But whom was I going to tell? My few friends were already part of my church groups. How did I get into a conversation with my dad about Jesus? Was I curious about whom he thought Jesus was, or did he ask me about the rally? What did it mean to be Jewish? I thought everyone needed to know Jesus, if they didn't know him already. It was only natural that I'd want to share something that I loved with someone I loved. The end of that discussion with Dad was traumatizing. "I don't need Jesus!" The absolute power behind his words continued to bellow with, "I'm a Jew, and Jews don't need Jesus. We go straight to God." I had no recourse, no comeback, no idea what just happened. Not until many years later did I realize how that encounter stunted my growth, tongue-tied my witness about Jesus, and affected my ability to talk to men.

I don't pretend to know the facts—not even a hint of the complete truth. I am the daughter of a wannabe detective dad like in *Dragnet* or *Perry Mason*. My probing personality gets overwhelming at times. I've got to dig and probe until I put the missing pieces in place. I wanted to hate my dad, but I felt sorry for him. Why didn't he ever have a "real" job? Was it alcohol and pot that screwed up my generation, or were we a product of our screwed-up parents? What was it about the 1950s and '60s that we didn't know when we were part of making history? They (those who dominated history and social reform) have analyzed our generation. They say we ushered in moral decline with bra burning, flower power, and free love. Or was it the brainwashing we got from television programs like *Donna Reed, Father Knows Best*, and *Leave It to Beaver*? The mothers always looked nice and made everything seem nice while treating the fathers nice. But no one can remember what the fathers did to bring home the bacon.

They were like kings in their castles, and their
wives were glorified servants. Didn't wives wait on husbands
hand and foot? Oh yeah, that was my mom and dad!

"Dottie, what are you doing out there in the kitchen?" He
seemed irritated if she wasn't in the living room, in her spot on
the couch, knitting. It wasn't long after she sat down that he'd either ask her for something from the kitchen or complain that her
steel knitting needles clicking against each other made too much
noise. I didn't think too much about whether my parents liked
each other or were in love. Our family didn't resemble any of the
TV shows we watched. Nor did our family reflect any image of
relationships I viewed from my church experiences. In fact, wondering why God was only a Sunday topic drove me inside myself
by the time I was a teenager.

And God said, "*What were you thinking, my dear women, when
you put me on a shelf to save me for a rainy day in your old age?*"

I remember sitting in that First Baptist Church of my youth,
drifting in and out of the sermon, contemplating my future. At
the ripe age of 13 and accountability, I wanted to be a good girl,
wanted to please God and serve Him on the mission field. I would
name my children Matthew, Mark, Luke, Faith, Hope, and Charity.
But I wanted to have fun. I liked dancing. I wanted to sing popular
Motown tunes. But I had already planned to be one of those gray-
haired old ladies sitting in the pews in the future. My adolescent
self chose to put God on a shelf that day at church in New Jersey, thinking I could put him on hold like a book at the library. I
wasn't thinking ahead about dues (dos or don'ts), being overdue
(doing it over), or late charges (penalties) that would be charged

to my account.

At 13, daydreaming about boys, sex, marriage, and babies, I wasn't thinking about my mother either. I had no interest in how and when she got married or how old she was when I was born. And now I wonder what I learned or heard or observed that generated my desire for babies. When I think that my mother was the age of my daughter now when I left home at 17, I'm shocked. My daughter, at 34, with a 17-year-old daughter, would make me, now 67, a grandmother. It's all too consuming to think about. It didn't happen. I'm not a grandmother now and may not ever be. Then what will become of all my journals and other memorabilia that my children will inherit? Will it make a difference if anyone reads them?

Do I seriously think my children—or anyone for that matter —would want to sit down with a pile of pictureless, handwritten books and read any single volume from start to finish? The last thing I want for my children or loved ones to do when I'm gone is sort through my stuff and determine if it's trash or worth keeping. If kept, what will become of it? Would it be more storage boxes on another shelf for 40 more years? I don't know what I hope to accomplish by writing and saving compiled sentences. What did I say with all those words? Better yet, what will the reader hear if they read them? Do words on a page make a sound just by being there? Are they just dead trees, ashes to ashes? Where is the beginning, and where is the ending? If everything ends the way it begins, if everything is circular and the day of our death is better than the day of our birth, then what's it all about, Alfie?

No. They are not dead voices when their thoughts are captured in words that become a message to the future. Wanting keeps us creatures hoping. I wanted babies more than I wanted a career. I wanted a father's blessing. I wanted to fill that hole in my *kishkas* (Yiddish for guts) that only God Almighty could fill.

Chapter 7: Adolescence, Trauma, & My Parent's Divorce
1St Husband (October 1968–July 1975)

I could hardly wait to graduate from high school and move to California. Plans and tickets were practically set in stone. I was leaving on a jet plane, no time for a fast train. My high school sweetheart, John, was already out there. We met in Mr. Greenspan's 9th grade general math class. I was 14; he was almost 17. "What are you looking at?" I had no idea he was talking to me, let alone why he'd ask me that. Was I looking at him? I couldn't see more than 4 feet in front of me because I would not wear my glasses unless absolutely necessary. I must have looked lost and, reflecting back, obviously confused. This was the second week of school, and my second math class, because I changed my schedule. Getting out of algebra before I got in too deep reflected doubts about my abilities. It was easier to give up. Because of Dad's frustration and impatience in helping me with my math homework in previous grades, I continued to hear his rebuffs: "Girls just aren't good at math. They don't need it anyway." The reverberations of his gender-role stereotyping further blindsided me into wondering where I was going.

Originally, I dreamed of going to college and becoming a physical education teacher. That did seem silly, though, since I was a short, pudgy girl wearing glasses with Coke bottle lenses. The financial situation for higher education didn't add up. There was no extra money in my immediate or extended family. No one ever talked to me about scholarships or grants. Changing my track from college to business afforded better odds at calculating and recalculating my budgeted income. After school I'd work as a file clerk at the AAA Auto Club. During the summer, I was a waitress. I spent hours reading and writing to help pass the time.

The first memorable thing I wrote was trash. It was a twisted tirade of teenage fantasy mixed with rebellion. Reading one trashy book set me off on a rebellious streak of ungodly thinking, writing about sex with foul language. I can't remember it all now, but my mother's reaction is permanently planted in my brain. She found the notebook I wrote it in, read it, and tore into me like a nun on a witch-hunt. How could her Bible- thumping Baptist baby think up such awful stuff and actually write it down? She punctuated her accusing judgments by admitting she'd listened in on my telephone conversations with my boyfriend, John. I don't remember what I wrote. I might have copied whatever it was that she read. Ah, the power of the pen and the spoken word.

Some of it was mere puppy love or maybe simple infatuation. Some words were ignorant manifestations of secret desires, fears, and frustrations. I'd been accused and judged guilty for my thoughts. I obeyed the other rules: be seen and not heard; if you have nothing nice to say, say nothing; do as I say, not as I do. If I'm judged guilty and serving the sentence, why hold back from the crime?

I practiced writing more than speaking, which should make me a better writer than speaker by now. Spoken words come too fast, before I have a chance to think about them. In person, they can come out like spit or vomit. Words can do more harm than good. I've uttered plenty of them with little care, little thought. Having a big ego and a big mouth adds up to disaster. Dad used to say, "You need to think before you speak." That didn't make sense to me, because speaking was part of thinking. If I were unable to think, I would not be able to speak at all. The act of writing forces you to search for words. Words slow down with writing. The words have to show the tone, the mood. The fuller meaning behind the intent is carefully thought out. And if, at first, you don't like them, you can take them back, erase them, or rewrite using better words.

Rewriting often feels like my Groundhog Day. I see shadows in things I've written that reflect like a recurring dream. In my teens, I'd often wake up in a sweat and rush to the dresser mirror to look at my teeth. I dreamt they were broken. Maybe it was the gunk built up from sleeping with my mouth open. Maybe they ached from sucking my thumb with tenacity. All I know is that I had the dream several times before I crashed into the old-fashioned claw-foot bathtub in the tiny bathroom of our apartment on Massachusetts Avenue, just before Easter, the spring before my 15th birthday.

John and I had been dating for a year. Our first official date was at the roller- skating rink in Ventnor, not too far from his home. Riding the bus to that end of the island meant leaving the ghetto apartments of the inlet and arriving at the other end of the point, where giant homes lined the beachfront.

John and his non-practicing Catholic family lived in Margate. His parents seemed to be friends; they had been through a lot together. His mother was from a horse ranch, and his dad was a farmer. Both of them were from Vineland, New Jersey. (An odd coincidence-the same place my paternal grandfather was from.) They moved to the shore, started a concrete business, and raised seven children, John being the oldest. They were hardworking country people adjusting to the city, living in a big, old house on a side street to the beach, driving a dump truck by day and a Lincoln Continental (with suicide doors) by night. They weren't exactly the model couple raising a God-fearing family, but they seemed to belong to me. They took me in, and I wanted to be part of their large family. I wanted to make my own large family. I believed that if I had a chance, I could do it much better than my parents, or even John's parents, for that matter.

John's father owned the concrete business that his four sons helped keep afloat. This Italian father set them up financially, teaching them a trade, but verbally beat them up with phrases like "henpecked," "chickenshit," and "sissy." On the surface, it seemed like he abused the boys and took advantage of them. John, taking the brunt of the beginning hardships of the business, decided to quit school and join the navy. If he enlisted before his 17th birthday, he'd avoid the Vietnam draft and shorten his service time. Even though John dropped Mr. Greenspan's math class and then quit high school altogether, he eventually got his GED and became a successful electrician in Silicon Valley. He worked for Omron Systems around San Jose, California, in the '70s. They dealt in banking and automation. I'll always wonder if that first resume I wrote for him after he got out of the navy launched him into an electronic gold mine.

One Saturday night, John was not coming over to pick me up. I wanted to go out, down to the other end of the island, to be with him and his family at their house. Why exactly my father was upset, I don't know. He wanted to know why I didn't have my friends come over rather than going out so much. "Are you ashamed of your home? Something wrong with inviting people here?" He made it clear previously that he wasn't exactly impressed with my boyfriend when he came to pick me up for dates. I gave them opportunities to get to know each other as John sat in the living room with my father, waiting for me. But the last time they spoke, Dad was rude and not very hospitable. As plain as the words on this page, I remember answering my father's question saying, "Maybe it is not the house but the people in it." I remember the layout of our house and running down the long hallway to the bathroom. I'd hoped to lock myself in, because my father was chasing me. What I said really must have struck a nerve, because he was furious. I know my teeth hit the bathtub, but I can't remember if he hit me or if I slipped on the rug and fell into it. Over time the hurt and resentment clouded my perception of the truth. The pain isn't based on the facts or concrete events but on the last thing I remember. I can still see my bloody mouth and broken tooth. The scars, the repressed thoughts, unconsciously seep up to the surface every year on the anniversary of the event.

I'm sure many neighbors heard me that March night when I left the house. To this day, I'm confused about what exactly happened. There is no Kodak moment for proof. Screaming, I ran out of the house and around the two buildings that led to a half-block street behind my house and banged on the door of my grammar school friend. Her parents were more upset about the blood I dripped all over their living room carpet than my home life that night. I don't remember what I told them, but I called John on their phone. I wanted him to come down to the inlet and get me, take me away from all this. It was because of him that my father was upset. Maybe my dad had been drinking. After that, I don't remember when he wasn't intoxicated.

As brief, painful, and truthful as the conversation was, that traumatic night in March was the last time I talked to my dad in that apartment we called home. John did come down to the inlet. My mother insisted that I not go with him but come back into the house. My father wanted to talk to me. He tried to apologize for what happened.

After he added an exclamation of "but" to his discourse, I continued to hold my bloody mouth shut. He moved out a few months later, and my parents divorced. Years afterward, when my father and I were able to talk about Jesus and my boyfriend, John, I forgave him. It wasn't easy for my father, growing up with a sick father and an immigrant mother. He didn't know how to be a father to me, much less a teacher. Telling me to think before I speak is like telling a kid to tie their shoe without ever showing them how to do it.

No longer finding solace in made-up boyfriends and forbidden pleasures, visions of the future danced in my head. At 15, tired of escaping into fantasyland and replaying the tapes of my imaginary characters, settings, and dialogues, I started writing. I replaced the fantasies with daily letters I wrote to my boyfriend,

John, my soldier boy who joined the navy and went away. I called him my "Johnny Angel," after the song by Shelly Fabares.

These may have been the beginnings of my daily exercise in journal writing. Letters to my lover. Letters from the inner me to an unseen, invisible connection to another life. A life with someone I hoped and dreamed would understand and love me unconditionally. I trusted John enough to pour out my words as if my life depended on it. Keeping them in my head was no longer possible. Eventually, the writing stopped, and we had to communicate in person, on the spot, in real time and real situations. If only we could have remained pen pals, if only we'd been able to keep writing each other, we may have remained friends.

Years later I realized how I'd replaced my private conversations with God with intimate conversations with a man.

So my writing career probably started as many writers' had in the old days, by letters. I wound up with his collection of letters from me after he got out of the navy. He'd kept every one I'd sent him, and I kept all he'd sent me, four or five pages—maybe more —each day. My mother kept those letters in a box in her attic for years with the plastic rose from a 5-foot Valentine. (I'll never forget how John carried that giant Valentine display card from Lit Brothers Department Store, down Atlantic Avenue to Arkansas Avenue, just for me.) I wish I'd kept all those letters I wrote to my first love. I wonder what I wrote about. School, my parents, his parents? My thoughts and feelings about life? Him? God? Questions about our future, about God's plans for our lives, and how many babies we'd have? What I was reading, studying, or sewing that day, that week? Did he write about boot camp, the chow hall, the cold weather in the Great Lakes?

I wanted John to be my everything when I left home to be with him. Maybe I wanted to possess him. I thought love meant he'd totally belong to me, and I'd belong to him. Whatever he was thinking or planning was part of my life. "Tell me. I want to know." I wondered about our future, his plans for when we'd get married and have kids. "But you get so disappointed when it doesn't happen."

In 1967 John planned for me to live with him in California after I graduated high school by clearing the way with my mother's approval. My father married his second wife that year and was not involved in the decision or plans for my future. John found us an apartment off the navy base in Mountain View, California, and encouraged me to transfer jobs from AAA in New Jersey to the auto club in San Jose. Saving and planning for my big break from home to join him included the responsibility for the payment book of a 1963 Pontiac Grand Prix. John purchased it in New Jersey and then drove it to California, where he was serving elective duty in the navy at Moffett Field. And he promised we would get married eventually. What did I know of marriage? I was unaware of the backlash of my parents' divorce. Later, their divorce would prove to be another rung on the ladder ascending my family tree.

Chapter 8: California Dreamin' And God's Not Dead

L ooking back, there was so much I didn't understand in 1968 when I left home and went to California. Things were far more complex than I realized. Take Vietnam. Not until I finally got around to getting to college (25 years later) did I learn that the Vietnamese helped the US intelligence operations in fighting the war. The US promised the Vietnamese safety and land for risking their lives for US soldiers. When I watched Born on the Fourth of July with Tom Cruise, I heaved tears of profound grief. The memories of proms, favorite songs, guys my age joining the service— God only knows what happened to them. Patriotism, pride, and my ignorance hit me with a wake-up call that filled me with sorrow and regret. I felt as if I could explode.

Before John went overseas in November, I persuaded him to marry me. "What if something were to happen to you? I'd not only be alone, but I'd be alone without your name." He agreed. A judge married us in his chambers that October in California. If it weren't for the Kodak memories, I might not remember wearing a purple herringbone wool suit and a white, frilly blouse. A squadron friend, John, and his wife, Linda, were our witnesses.

John and I often entertained some of the guys from his navy squadron. We had parties at our apartment, and many weekends a few guys would come over and hang out. We'd smoke pot, and I made dinner. We organized outings, camping, motorcycle rides, and trips to the beach. I recall a hunting trip when we drove to Oregon, and Tom, a troubled friend, came along. He was around often. One night he stayed over at our apartment because he was messed up on drugs. Someone said it was chocolate mescaline. When we left him in the living room and went to bed, I felt terrible and wanted my husband to help him. I thought I should or could fix him. My heart said he needed Jesus, but I was too messed up to put that into words for any man. That picture comes up in my mind, and I see how vulnerable and sympathetic I was and realize I must maintain boundaries. I felt pity and didn't recognize the emotion. Helping him find himself became some kind of mission for me.

My husband and Tom shared a living space off base in Okinawa, their last tour of duty. I suspect now that what I didn't know at the time is what troubled Tom when he spent time with us. Six months later, another navy friend let something slip because he thought I already knew. (As if that wasn't bad enough, this big-mouth guy was going to buy the Grand Prix I helped pay for that brought John from the East Coast to the West Coast.) During an evening of pot smoking, I maneuvered through the group sitting on our apartment floor, excusing myself in baby talk, saying, "koo-me." "She knows? You told her?" JD asked.

Later, after everyone left, I asked John what JD was talking about. My husband tried to rationalize his living arrangements in Okinawa with Tom and a Vietnamese woman named Kumiko (pronounced koo-MEE-ko). "Lots of guys had girlfriends over there," he said, trying to justify his actions. "She wanted to come back with me." Not totally surprised, but shattered all the same, I had to ask him, point blank, "You mean you lived with her, used her, knowing you'd leave her there to come home to me? How could you?" The hippie counter culture was all around me but I could not embrace free love and world peace. I had friends while John was overseas but I didn't have sex with any of them.

A recurring dream I'd had was that John would not talk to me. It wasn't like he was silent in the dream, but he wasn't saying anything to me. I'd be in the room with him, hearing him and not being able to understand what he was saying. I couldn't hear him tell me he loved me.

I started having nightmares of getting killed on some California highway on the back of John's Honda 750 custom chopper motorcycle with extended forks. I had a million reasons to go away but just needed one good one to stay, like Lady Gaga. I don't know what would have kept me with him. I was scared and angry — not that I would have admitted I had problems even if I recognized them. Having compulsive/addictive behavior's wasn't even a popular concept or phrase. I was trying to cope in an uncomfortable environment. I wasn't aware of the struggle within my spirit. My early religious training clashed with my outer lifestyle choices throwing me off balance. I feared I was crazy because I thought about God all the time and couldn't talk about Him. Literally or figuratively, if I were sick in the head and if people really knew me, they might lock me up. John said I should go home to my mother when I said I was leaving him. He thought I was merely homesick for my family. I didn't want to go home to Mother. I wanted to get away from him. I wanted what I wanted. If I wasn't getting it, I could move on. I was a selfish, rotten kid trying to get through adolescence. I was caught in the sexual revolution and revolting against authority. Or did I just want to get away from myself? (If only I could have been born a boy.)

Little did I know then that I was already locked up in my mind. When I decided to shut up about God and shut Him out of my life, I had nowhere to go. I used up the first person I loved. Instead of experiencing a Christlike life with John, I abused him, verbally and physically. His strong, lean, muscular body took it without retaliating. Lord knows what effect I had on his heart. Once, in that New Jersey Baptist Church, he sat through the service with me. Directing my eyes to the front of the altar, to the big writing that said, "Ye must be born again," he asked, "What does that mean, up there?" I don't remember what I told him. I don't know if I even knew how to explain it. Maybe I didn't really understand myself. It never occurred to me then that he didn't know how to receive Jesus into his heart. It never crossed my mind that God would save him then and there and that he could be the godly, missionary husband I wanted. Was that my vision or God's for me? But God didn't put me on a shelf, even if I were in California, living in sin. *Time* magazine ran an article titled, "Is God Dead?" I had to think about it. I had to think really hard, because I was busy getting stoned and fat.

I was expected to go to college after being only the second high school graduate in our family in over 40 years. Isn't it amazing when you wake up and can thank God because you realize it was all just a bad dream? How much more amazing is it when you wake up to reality and discover you were spared some frightful, nightmare life? My addictive, abusive behaviors manifested in food, alcohol, and pot to such a degree that I hated myself and ran away. Even running away would become a pattern. Didn't I run away from my hometown? My parents? Or did I run away from all that I was afraid of becoming? I ran away from John because of the motorcycle. Well, not completely true. I ran away because I thought I could see the future. I wanted babies, and I wanted them now.

"We're not ready. We have time," he would say.

"But I thought that's why people got married. That's the point of sex," I'd say. "If I can't have babies with you, I can have sex with anybody."

"You don't mean that," he'd say.

"Why not?" I'd ask. "It's okay for men to have sex and not have a commitment, why not for women?"

I burned my bra and stopped shaving my armpits. I turned 21 and went out on my own. I packed up the 1964 Chevy Impala my brother left in California after he and his girlfriend's short visit a few months earlier. Driving from San Jose to Anaheim was gutsy. With a chip on my shoulder, I stomped around, disappointed that my first love, my first husband, cheated, lied, and didn't want a family. I figured whoring around was just hippie power. Still strung out on pot, I was tied to another tether without knowing it: God seemed to be chasing me. I prayed for help, someone to talk to, some relief from my self-destructive trip to southern California. "God, if you are real, if you're there, reveal yourself to me." He answered me in a thrift store. One book stuck out 2 inches farther than the rest. Its title was the answer to my question—*How I Know There is a God*—and I knew God had bent down to answer me. A man of God came to where I worked a few days later. He was selling sides of beef out of a freezer truck. After asking the boss if he wanted to talk to this salesman, I had to tell the guy we weren't interested. He gave me a second calling card with a gospel message on it and asked if I'd be interested in hearing about the Lord. I thought, as a Baptist, that I knew everything. I took his card, but it wasn't until days later that I realized God had sent a messenger.

This salesman, Michael, took me to a Bill Gothard seminar called Basic Youth Conflicts, which was a Christian gathering for getting a foundation for a Christ-led life. The speaker spent one session talking about marriage and divorce. I didn't know it was called conviction when I wondered if God was trying to tell me to go back to my husband. I thought I was going through a grief process and that I'd eventually get over it.

This was all very amazing. What more could I have received? I asked for a sign and I got one—three, in fact. Less than a month later, back in my hometown, I had a dream and saw an apparition. It seemed like Jesus himself had his hand extended to me. I was awake, sitting up, asking, "Who are you?" Jesus wouldn't come to meet me face-to-face.

Chapter 9: 2nd Husband
(September 1975–July 1993)

Did you ever wish you could start all over? Take something back? (What if I had acted on what I thought I heard God say to me at the Christian conference?) I knew Scripture said that God didn't like divorce. But here I was, and it took all of my strength to break away from John. It hurt like hell. (If I really knew then what I wanted and had trusted God to trust the man who I believed God put in my life, then would I have been happy?) If I hadn't been a stubborn, selfish, rotten kid and taken John's advice to go home to Mother for a while, things might have turned out differently.

Six months after leaving John in northern California and screwing around in southern California, I went home to Mother. I had to share a bedroom with my mother's baby. The irony of being back in New Jersey with my mother, her new husband, Gus, and their new baby made me angry. I left my husband because he didn't want a baby. I tried to drown the emotions in alcohol and marijuana. I had dreams of running and being chased and an apparition that an angel came to me. I dreamt I was walking around a complex of white buildings. Three times I passed a certain spot on the path where I experienced a sense of weightlessness, as if I were being carried over a sinkhole and set on the other side. I woke up in a sitting position, with my hand reaching out and up. "Who are you?" I heard, and woke up. At first I thought I saw Jesus. He was stretching His hand out toward me. Now I believe that what I saw was an angel.

I got a job in New Jersey, attended some evening classes at the junior college, and hoped that Jesus still loved me. John used to tell me to remember that he loved me. I wanted him to come after me. I wanted him to apologize, profess his undying love, and tell me we should have babies. When he finally called me at my mother's, I wanted to avoid talking to him because I didn't want to cry anymore. I didn't want to be disappointed if he didn't say what I wanted to hear. He tried to apologize ... sort of.

"You wouldn't be doing this if it weren't because of what I did," I heard him say, softly and controlled.

"It doesn't matter now. Don't call me anymore," I remember saying, ending the conversation before the tears came.

Days later I got a phone call from Tom. After his discharge from the navy, he returned home to Minnesota. Eight months after his discharge, he went back to California to visit his old friends and discovered that I had left John. I wonder now what Tom expected when he talked to John about why I left. He didn't waste much time contacting me in New Jersey. Tom talked to one of my friends in California and found out where I was living. Mikki and her husband, JD, who was also in the same squadron, also knew about Kumiko in Okinawa. So when I got Tom's phone call at my mother's house, I cried on his shoulder. He thought he knew all about my first husband. I guess he heard a lot about me and my relationship with John when he lived with John in Okinawa. But when Tom decided to pursue me for his own, my future sperm donor thought he was getting a different woman. He must have thought I wouldn't be so unhappy if I were with him. "He doesn't love you. After what he did to you? Come on. Just come to Minnesota. Things will be better here. Just come to Minnesota." His tone was reassuring and coaxing. "I'll take care of you. Anything you want."

"I want babies," I told him. "I'm here, back home with my 40-year-old mother, her second husband, and their new baby. I'm the one who should have the baby."

"Come to Minnesota," Tom continued to persuade me. "Spend Easter here and maybe you..."

Easter was always a hard time for me. It's the anniversary of my blowout with Dad. The memories of that traumatic event are still with me.

Overwhelmed, my own life was more than enough to deal with in my state of mind. My father, who had remarried after I went to California, heard I had returned to New Jersey and decided to get back into my life. At least now we could go have a few beers together and try to talk. I remember asking him if he had been disappointed that his first child had not been a boy. He was flabbergasted that I'd ask such a question.

"Why would you ask that? What ever gave you thoughts like that? Did someone suggest that I was disappointed?"

I was afraid that he was getting angry, so I dismissed him with, "I read it was a Jewish thing, to hope that the first child is a boy."

I thought he was going to bust out loud, laughing. "Oh, don't start with that. I've told you, my mother isn't Jewish."

Once we got over the religious divide, I decided I could be friends with this man, but I didn't respect him as a father figure. He told me he was getting divorced (again). His second wife's name was Carol. He met her at John's apartment building. When I met her, I recognized her but didn't remember where I had seen her before. Dad said he was led to her apartment by an alien force. He saved her life. Why Dad was there and how he met Carol came to light years after the fact. I remembered seeing her in the hallway, by the entrance door of the apartment building. She was dressed in high heels, had jet-black hair teased high on top of her head, and had a beauty mark on the left side of her upper lip.

My dad thought he was a detective. Before he started following my brother around from nightclub to nightclub in the '70s, he was trailing me and trying to spy on me. He knew that my boyfriend, John, lived in the apartment building on Arkansas and Atlantic avenues. They both worked at the same department store

downtown. Weird, thinking my own father was a stalker. The store was within walking distance of the apartment. Evidently, there was another streetwalker who lived in the same apartment building. Why Dad was inside the building, looking for me, I'll never know. What did he intend to do if he found me? (We'd been very distant since my tooth and mouth incident. Was he trailing me before I had a clue? Come to think of it, there was a night in a motel when someone broke in and dumped the contents of my purse on the couch. Nothing was taken, and they left before John could get to the door, still putting on his
pants.) When my father busted in the door of another apartment, he found Carol, who was attempting suicide.

Dad was going through a painful divorce from Carol when I got married for the second time. After our wedding that September, Tom and I were at my mother's house with her husband Gus and other friends and family, including my father. My brother Steven, not yet married, got stuck escorting our father home that day. Steven was burdened with Dad's drinking problem. He had to deal with Dad creating scenes at different nightclubs where Steven's band was performing. One thing led to another. Fights and cops were involved. Getting help for Dad was Steven's mission. He tried to get him into a treatment program, but it never worked out and Dad would never follow through, so Steven washed his hands of it and gave up. He had to witness Dad's self-destructive behaviors eroding what little respect he might have had for him as a father.

My father's drinking worsened after his second divorce. After several years in and out of jails and hospitals, Dad met Grace. She was literally his saving Grace, his angel or messenger from God. Since I wasn't sure if he truly believed God existed, I wondered if God used Grace to get Dad to face his demons. He continued to drink. She continued to pursue a nursing degree. My brother remembered Grace and her children. When we lived at 20 S. Massachusetts Avenue, Grace lived in a basement apartment close to our family, but I didn't know her then. Steven used to hang out at

Grace's apartment. He helped her wash floors and entertained her two young children.

I remember seeing her walking down the street, pushing a baby carriage. There was one child riding inside and one walking outside, holding on with a little hand. Grace wore glasses and stood less than 5 feet tall. I saw the long, blonde hair on the child walking next to her and the brown-skinned baby inside the carriage. I didn't know Grace was only a few years older than I. If I was 15 then, she might have been 18. I'm not 100% convinced that she and my father ever got married, but they did have a child together. Their daughter was born the same year as my second son. Here again, my family likes to produce children when their children are producing.

In April 1973 I was visiting Minnesota. In June I moved in with Tom. We were married 2 years later, in September. John never pushed for a divorce, so I had to proceed with documents he sent me before Tom and I could get married. We had a church wedding in Ventnor, New Jersey, performed by an Episcopalian Priest. Dad liked this guy because he drank with him on my wedding day. We spent our honeymoon in Brigantine in a once-famous old hotel. A not-so-funny aside was overhearing waitresses the next morning describing my father, who had been hanging around the bar, talking about his daughter getting married and being in the hotel.

Tom and I returned to Minnesota and settled down in north Minneapolis in a 100-year-old house we bought to renovate.

Our first son was born prematurely in June. When our second child was born, we were still smoking pot. We drank and smoked cigarettes and pot as if they were our sustenance for life. But I wasn't happy. Remodeling was dirty and ate up all my salary from a pretty decent secretarial job. Tom was working at a foam-packaging manufacturer that didn't pay much, so he did remodeling jobs on the side. That slowed down progress on our house project. Tom was out of work for a while, transitioning to self-employment, and the financial strain started to erode our relationship. What was I doing 1,800 miles away from home, from my family roots? Oh, yeah! I wanted babies.

Still trying to create my ideal family, I faithfully wrote letters home and sent all the extended relations pictures of the children. My father and his new family were corresponding regularly as well. The fact that I named my firstborn son after my father and that he now had a child the same age as my second son fostered a new bond between us. My father's life continued to be an embarrassment to me. He had a young wife who had two illegitimate children, and now, in his 50's had a third child with her. I was challenged by my Christian faith to "be still and know God was in control." Thankfully, my little family and I had recently made some lifestyle changes. If I had not been active in a nondenominational charismatic theatrical church, I don't think I could have held my head up high when Dad announced they were moving to Minnesota. They said they couldn't handle all the changes that casinos and gambling brought to New Jersey. I wondered if Dad was still moving away from bill collectors. Grace was seeking a nursing job and her search eventually took them to Florida. However, while staying in Minnesota, I considered it a miracle that Dad attend church with me, once, and Grace's older daughter became a born-again Christian during an altar call at Jesus People Church.

Chapter 10: Turning Point

I n many ways, the book-writing process parallels having babies. Writing about the choices I made revolves around the children I so desperately wanted. Before conception, the insemination, the germination, the gestation, and, finally, the emergence of the young life is predestined. Writing feels like being pregnant: hungry and nauseous, fat and awkward, wondering and anxious about what's going to come out. Rewriting in hopes of not suffering too badly through difficult deliveries, query letters, and publisher rejections reduces some stress. No one talked about the post-delivery recovery. After people read my paper baby, some will like it and others won't. Then there is the attachment that is always a part of the mother, or the creator/writer. A silent child-rearing agony slowly trying to let go so your creation can live an independent life. Thank God for the times in which my babies were born. If I had been pregnant a generation earlier, there's a strong likelihood any of them, all three of them, and/or I would not have lived to write about anything. I've wondered if that dream I had three times in my mother's house, going around the white buildings and experiencing weightlessness, was a foreshadowing of the future like Footprints, in which God says, "It was then that I carried you."

The fact that my first child, a son, arrived 7 weeks early, proved to be a miracle. All his fingers and toes were accounted for, and all organs checked out as functional. He was yellow with jaundice because his liver wasn't quite

up to snuff, so he had to remain in an incubator until he grew some more. Child number 2, officially the middle child, was a breech birth. My physician at the time was supposed to be an expert at detecting breech babies before they got to the delivery room. When I was examined, it was determined my water had not yet broken. Turns out, the soft, spongy thing they felt was the baby's butt. The doctor was taken aback when I yelled at him as he proceeded to stretch the way clear to get the baby out. He goofed, and there wasn't time for a Cesarean section. Five years later, hopefully better prepared, I was full term with my third child. After I tried to get more comfortable on the delivery table and told the doctor I wanted to stand up, he told me the baby was posterior (face up) and he had to do a Cesarean section. I was 34 years old when my daughter was born. Three babies born, three difficult deliveries, and I decided I was not good at birthing babies and would never try again.

Children aren't born spoiled. Spoiling a child doesn't register as a negative thing while it's happening. Trying to give our children everything we wanted as kids might be spoiling us. We don't understand what it means to be a spoiled child until we try to give them everything and then they turn out much different than what we expected. How much does selfish lust rule our lives and shape theirs? Should we get everything we want? Thankfully, God gives us what we need. Even if we could come to terms with creating a little monster, could we live with what we get—a bad seed, a Teenage Mutant Ninja Turtle (a fighter with its head in the shell), not exactly mentally challenged or physically challenged, but an obvious reflection of what we created? Children learn from what they live with: too much attention (negative or positive), too many toys, not enough food (or too much food).

Everything that shapes them is a result of our influence on them. A keen, loving parent looking at these children might see the core of selfish existence reflecting back at them. Seeing self for self's sake gives us a glimpse of what God must go through. After all, He's given us earth, wind, and fire, soul, mind, and body, and we still spoil ourselves.

The spoiled child begets spoiled children. They can spoil like a rotten piece of fruit. What harm are they? My mother's husband Gus affectionately called me the rotten kid. If he had called me spoiled, I would have been angry with him for not understanding kids, since he didn't yet have any. Better to understand what they are not. They are not thinking of anyone except themselves. They aren't thinking about God, who sustains all life. It takes years to consider and believe that a higher authority can see over all the earth and all living creatures. It's very hard to fathom that God is more concerned about you than you are capable of being concerned for yourself. God must be waiting for some of us, like parents do, to snap out of it, grow up, and join the game of life so we can pass Go. Gus knew more than I did and that I wasn't ready to receive what he knew. His sensitive heart understood my mother's sadness and that she missed me terribly when I was 3,000 miles from home. So when Mother and Gus had their baby, they made a vow that this child would never leave home. Home, the house they lived in, would be the anchor that would keep their baby (Julia Dawn) close to their hearts and tied to her roots.

My anchor was pot. It made me stupid and kept me stuck. It might be a welcome alternative to pain and an escape for the end of life, but marijuana does not promote the desire for knowledge or to do good for others. The irony of my life going through birth pangs of an illegal drug like Pot becoming legal, mirrors my grandmother's existence through bootlegged Booz and prohibition. We, the people, are like the Hebrews, going around the mountain repeating the same cry and complaint about what we don't have and what we want. But the Jews mainly wanted food and water. In this century it's about more money, more power and more recreation - drugs, alcohol and sex. Some things never change so we repeat the Serenity Prayer. I'm thankful I inherited my Aunt Marc's 12" x 16" framed cross-stitched prayer reminder.

"God, grant me the serenity to accept the things I cannot change, the courage to change those things I can and the wisdom to know the difference."

Remembering back to when my firstborn was almost 4 years old and my second son was 2, - just prior to my Dad and his family moving to Minnesota - I put down pot for good. It was a turning point in that marriage. The older boy was watching us pass the joint, and it hit me like a blow to my chest. My heart ached that these children were high from secondhand smoke. That was in 1979, before they made public startling discovers about second-hand cigarette smoke. My oldest son was attending a day care at a church nursery school. One of the workers, Jennifer, attended a large, nondenominational church downtown. The Jesus People Church met in the old State Theatre on Hennepin Avenue, in the heart of a thriving metropolis. How it all happened that I shared some family stress with her and she invited us to church is a blur. I mainly remember her saying that she led my son to accept Jesus into his heart. Now that I think of it, she could have led him anywhere. He was later pinned the most gullible child in his class. His grandmother once innocently announced as an excuse for her raspy voice, "I have a frog in my throat." My son climbed on her lap, demanded, "Let me see in there," and poked around her mouth.

We went to that downtown church for 6 years. I didn't want to just attend. My children needed the Sunday school teaching, and I wanted to be their teacher, but I didn't think I knew enough. That's funny. Back in California, when that stranger invited me to Basic Youth Conflict's Seminar, I declared in my hardened heart that I was a Baptist. I knew it all already. So why did I feel my life was on the wrong track, going nowhere? I believed God would provide someone to see me through then, and He was trying to communicate with me now. After all, God doesn't start things He isn't going to finish. He knew what He was doing when I was born.

He doesn't make mistakes. It's because of my mother's mother, my grandmother Rose, and her prayers that I wound up in the Baptist Church. I'm convinced my grandmother's prayers had a lot to do with where I am today. Intercessor prayers for my children would come from remaining family ties and church prayer partners.

Tom went along for the church ride after our son's nursery school teacher convinced us to go to that big, inner city church. Three times a week, we fellowshipped, met with believers in a home group, and partied less with secular friends—at least I did. Tom was leading a dual life and growing unhappier as the months went by. He knew about my spiritual roots, referred to me as a "Jesus freak," and would jest about my Jewish heritage. His childhood experience with church and God were superficial. The closer I got to God, the more content I was in my spirit.

Change happens on the outside when we change on the inside, and people around us are either good with it or uncomfortable. Tom was so busy remodeling the house on the inside that he didn't recognize God's hand when He offered it on the outside. We were broke, and this old house needed a new roof. I had quit my job to raise the boys, and so I applied for grants and low-interest loans. Funds were only available to low-income families for home renovations. We just barely met the qualifications for a free roof—a grant—and I'm convinced it was by the grace of God. Tom thought it was a joke when I said, "God put the roof on our house." Remodeling was never going to end for him. Bills continued to pile up, and even miracles like free government money and a new roof were hard for him to credit to God.

In 1982, while I troweled the new cement sidewalk in front of that 100-year-old house, I flashed back to my first husband. The kids were little, and I sensed something rotten in the state of Denmark but couldn't put my finger on it. Attempts to work together with my second husband as a married unit taught me a valuable lesson in life: If you think you are trying to help someone and they get angry or defensive, it might be that they don't think you are helping. In fact, they didn't ask for help, so your interference is a put-down. It's as if you said, "Here, let me do it. You are doing it wrong, you dumbass." I thought I was helping him by offering advice, planning, and setting goals. He would agree with me and then change direction midcourse when he felt uncomfortable, leaving me bewildered.

Emotional disconnection is a subtle protective device and seemed to be Tom's defense shield. I poured my energy into the children. It was as if they only had one active parent. I made a few extra dollars providing day care for neighbors and getting sewing work by word of mouth. Keeping up with two energetic young boys' roller-skating, ice-skating, Little League, karate, and church activities was a full-time job. It was difficult trying to stay on a very tight budget. We lived in an older, not very safe, inner-city neighborhood around a large, active park. I was weary from constant vigilance. We needed help. We needed advice on remodeling, finances, our marriage, and the changing society that put "his needs" and "her needs" in a state of topsy-turvy.

There were too many problems in my life giving me headaches. Some days I would lie down and put a wet washcloth on my aching forehead, hoping sleep would take over instead of resorting to drugs. But sleep didn't provide solace when another recurring nightmare woke me up in a confused state of mind. I'd wake up forgetting where I was. We had rearranged rooms, walls, and floors in that house for years, and I knew every nook and cranny, every pipe and wire, every brick and block. In the dream, I was walking on the third-floor rafters, looking down onto the second floor, and seeing through that floor to the workings of the basement. In the fog of the ubiquitous remodeling dust, I'd glimpse my sons waving pipes likes swords and walking through walls with no drywall. Sixteen-inch-wide openings constructed of two-by-fours that didn't actually measure two-by-four was more math than I needed to know. The hammering, sawing, and drilling never seemed to end, and this dream came and went many times, leaving me breathless, with a view from the top.

Chapter 11: Life's A Puzzle, Not A Game

At this point, you/he/we/I put the past in perspective, checked the colors and the edges on the remaining puzzle pieces, and regrouped to fit everything together. Responsibility for another human being's life is not a game like Monopoly or The Game of Life, played by spousal pieces in the movable car and immovable real estate. At some point, it all seems to play out and end with winners and losers. My children's father played the role of poor sport. He blamed me for his business not paying the taxes. He claimed that if I had gone to work and given him more sex, it would have been so different. First of all, I'd have been worse than Frankenstein's monster or The Stepford Wives. I had quit my good-paying job to stay home with the boys. It was all I could do to get through the day's chores, putting on a good front for their sake. Keeping an organized, smoothly running house with little to no money takes brain-damaging power. Their father could not appreciate my talents. "I don't care if the house is clean," he said. "I just want a woman who will love me."

I'd respond with, "What does that mean? Can't you tell? I darn your socks, never let you run out of clean underwear, wash the car, cook decent meals. Doesn't it count that I am here? That I am dependable, reliable, honest, and loyal?" Evidently not!

Second, it was probably all a bad dream. I tried to tell him what I liked. Mayonnaise spread to the edges of the bread, a clean bathtub after his use, and a certain touch at a certain time. But he heard each specific request as a personal attack on his ability to do it right. After so many years, I gave up trying to communicate my wishes for fear of upsetting his delicate mood. He'd complain more frequently and retaliate with passive-aggressive behaviors. "If you'd love me more, I'd be able to work better. I wouldn't be behind in the bills. You expect me to be the man of the house, but you won't do what I tell you."

In my defense, I'd say, "What do you want me to do? We agreed that going back to work while there was a preschooler in the house wouldn't be fair to the child and wouldn't amount to much income after expenses." Those same lines, in varying degrees, were repeated over and over, in circles, for hours at a time. When I eventually got a job driving a school bus, Tom said it wasn't a real job. "You're off having fun while I'm trying to pay for all this for you."

"All this" was a modest house in a decent suburban neighborhood that we were able to afford after selling the albatross in north Minneapolis. It was a refreshing relief from our first 10 years in the inner city, remodeling a century's worth of headaches. We turned a repossessed triplex into a rented duplex, incurring way too much debt. During that time, I wrote an article for the local community rehab group about the blood, sweat, and tears of remodeling that eroded our marriage. The city paper got ahold of it and sent a writer to our house to take pictures and get more juicy details. I knew then that my career as a writer had been dormant. Journaling wasn't enough. My words were piled up, creating a mountain that I would someday have to climb over instead of going around and around. I was smoldering inside, slowly burning a quiet fuse set to ignite like a delayed firecracker.

Looking back, the puzzle pieces of the children's problems in school fit into the area of neglect. So much time going around the mountain could have been quality time spent with them. I felt so bad getting caught up in their
father's self-defeating, inflexible, self-pitying rhetoric that I wished I'd never gotten involved with him, and yet he was my

children's father. This was my life. What was God thinking?

> And God said, *"What were you thinking about when I was
> trying to communicate with you through my
> messengers?"*

Maybe my sons will blame me if they suffer terrible generational curses like impotence from maternal pot smoking during pregnancy. Maybe their own pot habits or addictions and, possibly, negative relationship issues with women will be my fault. They are not even married yet. They still haven't come to terms with their parents' divorce. My oldest son, while processing his parents' divorce and mother's third marriage, tried to live with me and my new husband. It lasted 2 weeks. His hunting hound of 7 years had been his crutch, a shoulder on which to mourn the loss of his mother. When he finally dumped his anger about the divorce, we realized the dog had replaced not only me, but also the puppy he had as a toddler. I was responsible for sending Deak, an English pointer with gentle manners, to the farm to live with another family because two dogs and two children were more than I could handle. His festered pain spilled out over the loss of that dog and a front tooth while playing with him when he was 2 years old.

My second son cried a lot as an infant. He was an unexpcted conception and his birth disrupted his father's deer- hunting plans. He displayed a sensitive spirit and strong will that might account for his hyperactivity. I anticipated his moods to alleviate everyones stress and was told I coddled him. He seemed to inherit a victim mentality, so he blamed me for everything from his dad's lack of money to his football injuries. I caused everything. I was the most powerful person in his world when he was 13. Not until he was 23 did he start to think about taking responsibility for anything, until several car accidents.

After the divorce, our sons were very angry and unkind. Tom moved in with his brother and wife in another suburb. The boys were 14 and 16 and didn't see much of their father. When he did come around, he was uncommunicative, sulking, or extremely moody and negative. My daughter was 9 and too young to put her feelings into words, but I sensed the pain she felt from her father's words or lack thereof, and the anger from her brothers' words. "Mommy, why can't our family be like *Little House on the Prairie*?" she asked, years before the divorce. She watched the show on TV. I never read Laura Ingalls's books, but I knew she meant that there were families who talked things over and lived in harmony. What happened to that vision of a godly husband, a half dozen children with biblical names, and a home much different than any I'd known? Didn't I deserve them? Didn't I believe I did? I believed in God and His goodness, but did I believe in myself?

When did I start to rewrite the stories in my head? How else could I escape but in my dreams, wondering if I were too old to believe in Prince Charming? My pride jumped from one marriage to another. My lust jumped into the hot frying pan, and now I had these little monsters scaring me into a corner. I felt trapped in regrets and pining for another chance. I wondered, if my first husband and I had had children, if these had been his children, would they speak to me the way these boys did? I doubt it. John had been a firstborn child. He loved his mother. He seemed to look after her and protected her. I sensed that she protected him from his father. He would have taught our sons to honor their mother, take care of her as a woman who needs what men can supply. As much as our generation fought for equality, the roles of husbands and wives were blurred between new attitudes and old values.

Tom and I had different upbringings. His dad had a steady job. He worked at the same 9–5 job in a factory until he retired at 65. They might have been lower-middle income, when we were just above poverty level. Tom lived in the same house in a suburban neighborhood his entire childhood. My family moved every couple of years, trying to avoid bill collectors. Our mothers had more similarities, though. Both were dependent on their older husbands, neither had a driver's license, and both made money on the side from sewing and other crafts. They catered to their husbands' needs. Asserting themselves and occasionally taking time for themselves was not looked on with praise but with scorn. How we were raised, I as a firstborn girl and Tom as the middle of three boys, played out in our own child-rearing skills. We didn't usually see eye to eye on how situations should be handled.

I woke up one morning, eyes opened to my marriage with my children's father, conscious of the me I was before children and the me I had become. For a brief second, a glimmer of clarity sparked a neuron in my aching head. My life seemed clouded over by drugs, alcohol, or other appetite diversions. Part of me was living in a fantasy. I'd lie down at night, pretending my husband was someone else. I pretended I was with another man, a man cloned from my childhood who I interacted with, the perfect man of my dreams. I woke up and cried before God to forgive me for committing adultery in my heart and not accepting the woman he created me to be. I asked for forgiveness for not accepting the man He put in my life, wondering who chose whom. My question wasn't "Who do I think I am?" but "Who do I think God wants me to be?" When I talked to God in the church of my youth, in 1963, and put Him on hold like an operator answering another call, I didn't consider that God never hangs up. The direct line to Him goes through dirt, sand, oceans, and lakes, from the garden to the desert, from beginning to end, with constant, consistent purposes that only seem like a coincidence to us mere mortals. Not until the student is ready will the teacher appear.

While slowly unraveling my Baptist beliefs after the birth of my first son, my Jewish roots started to show. The Jesus People Church fell apart the year after our daughter was born, and so did some people's relationship with God. Tom was disillusioned, but I was more determined to keep my family together. I felt sheltered and safe in the next congregation we joined. They taught and worshipped a form of Jewish Christianity. Northwest Christian Fellowship was our new family, made up of old friends from Jesus People Church and new nondenominational believers. Tom pondered with trepidation whether his wife was Jewish or Christian. How could she be both? And didn't one's mother have to be Jewish for the children to be Jewish? Then, if I am Jewish, does that mean my children are Jewish? I wonder, what part of this information upsets the enemy of God?

My maiden name was part Jewish. I named my first child after my father. Psychologically, I don't know why. I liked his name, and it was a way to honor him. My father, however, changed his last name from Berstein to Vann-Berstein. People used to ask me if I was Dutch. "No, French," I'd reply. Years later, when my mother and sister were discussing marriage licenses and who lied about what, Mother told me she always wondered if her licenses were legal. She said Marcelle Berstein and Smily Jack Vann were legally Bersteins. The missing puzzle piece: My father was ashamed and afraid of his Jewish identity (which he sometimes denied because his mother wasn't Jewish), so he tried to hide behind his name. He didn't need God or Jesus, I guess.

In my studies, I've learned that the rabbis declared that the religion of the children is determined by the mother because they couldn't prove who the father was but could see how the mother raised the child. That's my loose, unprofessional interpretation of the rabbis' teaching. I personally believe God made a covenant with Abraham, and the seed of the male determines the true identity of the child. Either way, I felt cheated out of a portion of my identity when I learned all this. I could have been closer to the front of the line all those years in school—a *B*, not a *V*—not to mention missing the Jewish view of God until I was in my 30s. I had to wait 26 years for the blood of my Jewish heritage to burst through my Baptist veins.

I felt like the living dead, because my life had reached another plateau, and I was trying to analyze every step that got me there. Playing detective, putting the pieces of the puzzle together after the murder, was second nature, like forensics. It's only logical to deduce the probable by working backward from the facts when the dead body is discovered. The clues traced to the murder are as definitive as OJ and Nicole's. You can't always do what you want. Just because you're grown up, even if you have money, power, or fame, that doesn't mean you can do whatever you damn well please. What about honor and dignity, loyalty and justice? My children have said that I should have been a lawyer rather than a teacher. I'm just looking for truth, nothing but the truth, justice, and the American way. I'm not my children's hero, and I'm not just their mother.

After the second divorce, when I was getting married for the third time, a new piece of my puzzled mind fit together when a friend asked, "Isn't it too soon to remarry? Aren't you just on the rebound?" I wanted to tell him, "Thanks, but I think I'm divorcing the rebound marriage from husband number 2." I didn't leave number 1 for number 2. I hooked onto number 2 because I left number 1. I was sicker than I thought.

I hadn't planned to get married again. After divorcing my children's father, I was hurt that he was so angry with me. I had been so angry with him for not keeping up with what I believed was his end of the marriage bargain. There was salary competition when I first moved to Minnesota and got a secretarial job that made more money than his construction work. There was confusion and misunderstanding between his concept of religion and mine. Deciding on how we would spend our lives together mushroomed from his creative genius remodeling an old house and mine on rearing God-fearing kids. We were rarely in sync about money, mood, or memories.

Our oldest child was 17, and I was in college, with hopes of getting a teaching degree so I could be self-sufficient. If this marriage taught me anything, it was that I gave up a career to be dependent on someone else to secure my financial future. I had hoped, or wrongly thought, that I could help him, save him from drugs and mental hassles, if he knew Jesus. I felt I was still taking care of him after our divorce by reversing the judge's decree so he could live in the house with the children while I moved out.

After two divorces, my thoughts and feelings about failure or defect overwhelmed my long days and even longer nights. Staying focused and centered on children and college were blessings but hard and lonely. I had a few friends, mostly from church, but none like a brother or a sister to confide in who would validate my feelings and straighten out my thinking. Believing in God and relying on Him for support are part of my core, but that doesn't negate the need for human companionship. I spent as much time as I could at church, fellowshipping with Christian friends and keeping active with my sons' high school experiences and daughter's middle school. I was determined to make it on my own. And then I met husband number 3, Clay, through a dating ad.

Call it coincidence, divine intervention, or a naive gamble, but I just happened to notice a dating magazine at the grocery store checkout. I was on my way to the college I was attending in Minnesota. My mother's friends in New Jersey were sending her newspaper clippings of singles looking for dance partners. I wondered if they had magazines like this in her community. There were pages and pages of single men and women, in different areas of the state, from all sorts of diverse backgrounds, and many included pictures. It was as if something inside me exploded. I knew I would answer the ad that echoed my soul's search to line up my father's Jewish roots and my Baptist upbringing.

His Ad:
DWM 46, Arden Hills, MN   - - Handsome, sensitive, divorced, young 46.
5'8", 180 lbs Jewish Christian. Waiting to write you a poem. Love talking and walking by lakes, drives to Duluth. I talk to God and He answers. You believe in Christ, 30-40 petite and cute. Love poems, music, holding hands and praying. Seek lasting friendship and love. Call or write and be blessed.

Chapter 12: *Leave This Chapter Out*

(In Mother's Own Words)

In response to reading my first draft in 2007 of
Life's a Puzzle and I Think I Lost a Piece,
Doris Mae Adams (Vann-Berstein) Gross, my mother,
wrote me the following:

F ound that "lost piece"?

We may never know 'til we meet our Maker. Perhaps not even
then.

I can only convey what I've come to realize in my 74 years and
from hearing stories of other friends and relations.

Men's world is ruled by that thing that hangs between their
legs.

Women's world is ruled by the desire to please (men).
It's been going on since the beginning of time.

Guess you realize your writing arrived today. I've now read it
a couple of times, and find myself confused, not knowing which
husband you're talking about and who's having the conversations
with whom.

I can feel the deep, underlying feeling of guilt on your part. I've
been there— several times—but I managed to get over it.

1st guilt: throwing your father out after 17 years of marriage. Although I was deathly afraid of him, my courage came after going
to work and meeting someone (Bill Galey) who treated me like a

princess and showed me a whole new world that I had not experienced.

Bill was not the first. I was "seeing" someone (who will remain nameless) the entire time I was pregnant with Steven. Your father was either too damn to know or too busy with his own little trysts.

2nd guilt: having had two illegal abortions and, after being thoroughly disgusted with myself for getting knocked up a third time, performing my own with a knitting needle, not caring if I lived or died.

3rd guilt: Gus's death. I should have known that he wasn't right. In hindsight I recall his tiredness—even pictures of him before his death, I can see he wasn't the same.

Let's get in the world of daydreaming. Imagine a phone call or letter arriving from the West Coast declaring no ties, curious of status, possibilities of a meeting, if for nothing else but heartfelt apologies from both parties. What would your decision be?

I've mentioned the guilt trips I've been on, but as I said, I've gotten over them. God will judge me when it's my time. I do believe if we confess our sins and ask forgiveness, it will be done. I've done this numerous times over the years.

I have only one regret, and let's face it, time is running out. An apology overdue by 58 years to Reginald Garner. Maybe time has run out for him. I may never know.

See, history does repeat itself. We both left broken hearts in California.

Think hard. Any regrets? I'm sure there are some you can't do anything about, but are there any that you can?

I'm sure you've heard me say, "Children are what the parents make them." I'm not pointing fingers; I'm reflecting on my own life. I was pleased when my mom and dad separated. I had always felt she deserved a much better life than he provided. At least with Joby, she had a roof over her head without someone banging on the door because the rent wasn't paid, living nights in the dark 'cause the "juice" was turned off because of unpaid mounting bills, and three square meals a day—not relying on Dad to maybe catch a fish so that we'd eat that night. She truly loved him up until the day she died, but I ask myself, *Would she have married him if she wasn't pregnant?* Then, to think that baby died a few days after birth. Then here's another tidbit: Sonny's "father" was not her first affair. Guess I was 7 or 8. She was playing "twiddlywinks" with Uncle Boo. I was an eyewitness, a thought-to-be sleeping child on the back seat of that old jalopy, parked near the ball field in Pleasantville, with the door of the passenger side open—he had very long legs. But the laugh was on them. I had already discovered masturbation and was having a party all by myself in the back seat without their knowledge.

As for my dad, I was happy for him, that he found his soul mate, a perfect match: sex-crazed barroom buddies. Hilda was good for him. If things didn't go her way, she'd beat the crap out of him. Maybe my mom would have had a better life if she'd been into fisticuffs.

By the way, I had found out years ago about my mom being "preggie" before marriage. The original marriage certificate had been altered to read one year earlier. Then, lo and behold—it must be a family trait—yesterday I was rooting through old shit in the attic and came upon her mother's marriage certificate. With it was a handwritten note (by my mom) that Dorothy (mom's sister, the firstborn of Maribelle and Thomas) had changed the date from 1910 to 1909. What does that tell you? And no, my marriage license is not altered. However, I did lie about my age.

I guess you can say I was running away too. Not a very stable home life. A mother who goes across country, gets pregnant, and has balls enough to bring her big belly back to Atlantic City, and a father who is dumb enough to take her back and even give the child his name. Not to mention that the biological father came to Atlantic City for a visit. Can you envision Finis and Bus getting drunk together?

Anyway, it was time for me to run. I had met my Prince Charming, and I didn't want to become the built-in babysitter. Now, as

I look back, they had screwed up their lives. Now it was my turn to screw up mine. I can say I was never as bad off as my mom, although I know for a fact I could have been, had it not been for Grand-Mère; i.e., food, money, and such. It took a number of years for me to realize there was a drinking problem. There were a few times I was ready to split. Can't remember exactly when those thoughts started, but it was after I went to work—realized I could pay the bills, I could save money, I could feel good about myself. I didn't have to be afraid of him when I'd come home from work and find him, still in pj's, lying on the sofa, watching TV. And there were numerous nights when he didn't come home at all. Anyway, that's when he got his walking papers.

I just remembered when my thoughts of splitting started. You were only 5 years old. That's when I told Grand-Mère, and she was behind me 100%. But she and Jackie cooked up that deal to go to Philadelphia and watch Sandy while Jackie was having Ronnie.

(NOTE: Mother didn't remember this clearly. She went to help Jackie with her first child. My cousin Sandy was born on my golden brithday, July 5, 1955.)

Chapter 13: How I Met My 3rd Husband

Answering a dating ad was not my plan. It was the least likely thing I'd ever do. Hadn't I decided to be absolutely alone? Wouldn't that be far better than spending another day with my children's father? What would it be like to live alone and be an independent, truly autonomous human being? Well, it's not possible. I had three children at the time.

My mother's friends were sending her clippings once a month of potential dating partners from ads they thought she should answer. Dance partners were targeted. They must have felt her loneliness. They all heard the story about how she reunited with Gus almost 30 years after dancing with him at the Steel Pier in her teens. They got married, and mother got pregnant at age 40. Gus had been married before, but they had no children, and he was the oldest of 10 siblings. When he passed away from a heart attack in his sleep after his daughter's 13th birthday, my mother and half sister lived 1,800 miles away—and a greater distance from me in their pain. Did her friends know how much she drank and slept her life away after her second husband's passing?

Mother would have been 60 years old when I noticed a personals paper at the grocery store. I was amazed that these ads went beyond the newspaper column and that an entire magazine with pictures was available. Did Mother have access to this kind of publication on the East Coast? What do women my age see in this?

Would I have the guts to respond if I expected my mother to? I wondered if I were more like Mom than I was willing to admit. Curiosity pulled me into the magazine, and I zeroed in on an ad that interested me. It read "Jewish believer." Well, if I were going to answer ... "oh Lord. Oh Jesus. God no." I knew I was destined to answer the ad, and if this guy were not for real, God would reveal that too. I didn't just start trusting in Him yesterday. I believed I was mild-mannered, God-fearing, humble, and extremely cautious.

My friend Jodi was so excited when my response letter to the dating ad generated a phone call from the DWM who was a Jewish believer, who claimed, "I talk to God, and He answers me." This man's response jarred my brain. When I prayed for my father to be saved, for him to accept Jesus into his heart, I didn't know enough to consider if he would stop being Jewish. If I were to become Catholic, I guess I'd stop being Baptist. My grandfather was Jewish, and as far as I could tell, that simply meant he was born Jewish. My grandfather's wife was born French. Later, this will all come together. God orchestrated a teaching about nationality and religion that defies coincidence and demystifies the possibilities of a Supreme Being who can choose the players He wants, the playing field He favors, and the length of the playing time. I didn't ask to be born. I exist because of love. If the two people who genetically formed my human existence didn't understand love or agree to that love, the God who created the dirt does. He planned the players, the playing field, and the playoffs.

Jodi was the only one who knew about the dating ad. I couldn't let my sons know what I was up to. They were already Daddy's bleeding-heart fans. He was emotionally inappropriate with them. Anything getting back to their dad to make him angry, to give him fuel to fan the fires of an ex-husband, would boomerang onto the children. They suffered through their time with him as he acted as the victim of a selfish, whacked, wanton woman who was never satisfied. Maybe it's true. Maybe I'm never satisfied.

I asked Jodi to act as a go-between for me and this dating-ad guy. I used her phone number to be contacted. She screened him, to some extent, so I could get his number and decide if I wanted to call him back. I did call him, and we planned to meet in Blaine at a pancake house for breakfast after my bus route. Driving a dump truck was on my bucket list, but for now I was a school-bus driver going to college, trying to make ends meet, when I met my third husband, Clay. He tells the story of how we first met at that pancake house for breakfast. He didn't know what to make of me in a jean jacket, black biker boots, and stringy dirty blond hair. "The potato pancakes are really good here," he suggested. "I don't do pancakes," I replied, trying to be funny. (I didn't know that potato pancakes were like *Latkes* and related to Hanukkah. I might have responded in a more politically or religiously correct manner if I had known.) He wanted to tell me he didn't "do" bus drivers, but he didn't.

After the initial anxiety of our first meeting, we talked about my answering the ad he had placed in the magazine. He said he had forgotten about the ad. It was free. He wasn't lonely. He had friends. I thought the next date should be a Christmas treat, so I suggested a local dinner theater performance of *Fiddler on the Roof.* I didn't expect to just date, but I wasn't planning to get remarried. Wondering about matchmakers in the play and God's way of intervening in our lives, I believed, if God was in this, that I'd grow in a third marriage, but it had to be as right as right could be for the third time. The third marriage strikeout could prove far worse than other sets of three in my life. Clay had been married once and had custody of his two preteen children. His life was in chaos, and his search for stability was through church, 12-step programs, and his poetry, similar to my search for a new lease on life. The similarities might have been red flags, but there were also opposite qualities that attracted us. Maybe I had the vision and he had the guts.

He went out to his Thunderbird, which had a broken driver's side mirror, to retrieve his box of poems. They were neatly typed and stacked in an 8x10 stationery box in the trunk of the car. He brought them into the restaurant, where he let me leaf through them and read his personal creations. My first thought was that I was reading my own writing. Either this was me or this guy was my soul mate. This was either corny or divine intervention. Either way, I was content to believe God was in this meeting.

"So, what do you think now about answering my ad? You were the only response I got. Why did you answer it?" His questions were rapid-fire.

"My dad used to say he talked to God and God talked to him. He's also Jewish, and he made it very clear to me that he didn't need Jesus." I tried to sound resolute.

"Have you ever seen *Fiddler on the Roof*?" he asked.

"Maybe, but I don't remember. I just like musicals," I told him. Clay chuckled at my remark.

Discovering that it was about a Jewish family, and that Tevye, the papa, talked to God and that a matchmaker was finding husbands for his daughters was like solving a Rubik's cube. How far will this divine meeting go? And as if he could read my mind, he asked, "Do you think you could love a guy like me? Just think," he said, "if this amounts to something, what a fantastic testimony it will make for the Lord."

Is it any wonder that I'd marry a third time or that I'd be married to a Jewish believer in the Messiah, Jesus? What an oxymoron. The idea of being married a third time was scary. I'd had three babies, and each time was not the expected natural childbirth. Three strikes in a ball game and you're out. I'd gamble on the sure bet that three hits were enough for me in the baby-making department. There is no magic number, unless you have a genie in a lamp. And I'm not given to magic or wishing in any way. Only prayers have power. So I was praying that if God would bless me with a third husband, I had to put Him first. Number three would be sold out for a Christ-centered life or it wasn't meant to be.

Then, if this part of my life reveals the fingerprint of the triune God, and He is sovereign, wouldn't you expect the person you loved and who loved you to want the very best for your life? If, in your heart of hearts, the very best was only possible serving the one true God of Abraham, Isaac, and Jacob, would you put all your efforts aside and trust God to be who He says He is? Of course, you have to be totally dedicated to spending time with Him. He is a jealous God. He wants your life. Your best is the most you can offer back to Him. Hasn't he already given us everything we need? Maybe not what we want, but surely every single need, large or small. If He would explain to us our strengths and weaknesses before we got into trouble, would we worship Him for the supreme King that He is? My husband, Clay, and I committed to spending our lives serving God before we had a clear vision of what that would entail.

May 8, 1994 – Mother's Day Poem

Are you my Mother?
You nurture me, help me grow.
Take care of me? Yes.
You take care of you? Best.
How you take care of you helps me
Take care of myself.
Honest words, dialogue, not monologue.
We can talk, and be quiet and still communicate.
You hold me in comfort,
I learn what I need. Who knows mothers best?
He who created them.
Helpers, these special women who know how to guide.
Then get out of the way for HIM to do HIS work.
Are you my mother?
Sometimes,
But in being before,
You are more now.
And I remember,
And it continues,
And I am grateful to my Father for you.
Susan, full of Grace.
Amen,
Love, Clay

June, 1994, Father's Day Poem

God is my Father. He is a great Daddy.
My Daddy is SO BIG.
He can see the whole world at once.
I can only see backwards.
When I was a little girl, my daddy's hand was the biggest.
I'd hold only two fingers as we walked. When he'd go away,
The smell of his tobacco and Cologne would stay.
I'd think of him: his play-acting, his funny voices,
His characters, his cough and eccentric choices.
I'd laugh within and wonder which car or motorcycle I'd see him in.
Then times and changes and I grew and I knew
More than my daddy from a woman's point of view.
But only my Heavenly Father saw the sensitive void.
For my daddy's regrets of being a Jew robbed my joy.
I honor my father and I'm grateful for his part in Gods' scheme,
For all my prayers will be answered as I dream.
If I'd been lost, my daddy would have searched for me.
He'd calm and quiet my fears and my tears.
My Heavenly Father searched the Whole World
For my lost sensitive spirit. He found me and planted me
In an interim garden where I'd be protected and nourished.
He planted me right next to you.
You who were remarkably familiar
And so astonishingly renewed to flourish.
Only my Father could choose my father.
Only my Father could choose for me
A Man of God who listens to his Father
And who has fathered by listening.
You will know the wonderful joy of the Father's love
When His own come back home and embrace Him.
His love endures forever.

Chapter 14: 3rd Husband

(November 1995–February 2009)

C lay and I dated for a year and lived together under scrutiny from both our churches and our children. Our respective communities were 40 miles apart, causing a wide gap between church friends and the children's schools. We got married by a messianic rabbi in the church Clay's best friend, who had led him to Jesus in the 1970s, attended. At this crossroads of my life, I'd come to view marriage and divorce as a legal contract, binding until someone breaks the deal. I wanted to believe that this guy was sold on Christ and would act like it. I tried as hard as I could to put all my biblical knowledge into force and exercise my choices to line up with what God would want me to do in another marriage. I attended a Christian college and graduated with a bachelor's degree in secondary education, with a focus on language arts. I worked the next three years in non-traditional teaching environments and paid off my student loans. We became members of a nondenominational church, co-laborers for Jews for Jesus ministries, and home Bible study group leaders, and we attended major Bible conferences. We were part of a Christian Classic Car Club. We volunteered at crisis hotlines and deliverance prayer meetings. But none of that guarantees you get to pass Go and collect $200. You can do everything right and someone else crashes into your car. You can be in the right place at the wrong time. It seemed like we were on the same page most of the time, headed in the same direction: getting closer to God and what He wanted for our lives. Before the end of my third marriage, we had been doing live and taped radio and cable TV ministry broadcasts. God had our attention, and the ministry outreach functioned with the help of a few dozen supporters.

As an evangelist cleverly disguised as an insurance agent, Clay was able to procure multiple properties and dozens of vehicles while living 3 months a year in Florida. Because of this, I was able to travel across the states and to Israel. I reconnected with my brother and father and shared time with them, discussing our Jewish roots and belief in God. Clay developed a close relationship with my brother while we were in Florida the very first time. He enjoyed Steven's passion for music, cigars, and Corvettes.

"Does your brother know what it means to be Jewish?" Clay asked. He didn't waste much time learning about one's position on God. The connection between what you have here on earth and what your future holds in the hereafter bridged any gaps for Clay to cross lines of religion and nationality. "No, I seriously don't think he gives it much thought." I told him. "He'll tell you he is French."

He thought of Steven as a little brother, and after meeting my father and hearing about my witnessing opportunities gone sour with him, Clay was challenged in his heart to connect with my dad before the opportunity for salvation was too late. So when Dad got sick and his nurse wife told us she didn't think he had much time left, Clay and I planned to drive from Clearwater to Ocala to pay our last respects. Being a bold, pushy salesman, Clay pestered my brother Steven to make the trip with us. "Why would I want to do that?" Steven asked. "He has never made an effort to come to see me. And he'd be a pain in the ass if he did." At the last minute, my brother had a change of heart. "What the hell. I guess I don't want to regret not saying goodbye to the rat bastard. I don't know if you're a pastor or a rabbi, so I guess we've got all our bases covered."

After several hours cruising Florida highways in the 1968 white

Cadillac, we visited a frail, skinny, old man of 78, wheezing and on oxygen. "Why are you here?" he asked. "Why now are you finally coming to visit me?"

It wasn't like we all got together as a family for holidays. I was living in Minnesota, Steven was in Florida, and we still had family members in New Jersey. We were still a broken family, and no one was making an effort to mend us all together.

Except for Clay. He empathized with our shattered family. His family had written him off as dead when he announced to his Jewish relatives that he understood and now believed that Jesus was the Jewish Messiah. They were doubly upset when they learned that he had led his mother in a sinner's prayer before she died. He was confident she accepted Jesus when she told him, "What could it hurt for me to believe the way you do?"

Clay probed and pried with salesman skills to determine if my dad believed that Jesus was God's son sent to earth to die for all of our sins. With his usual argumentative attitude, Dad barked at us, "Alright already, so Jesus is God. Now what?"

As if to close the deal, Clay said, "You might not have another opportunity to bless your children, so you're going to put your hands on each of them and bless them in the name of the Lord."

At this point, Dad looked exhausted and was stretched out on the couch. He reached out his right hand to Steven. Clay said, "Put your hand on his head and say, 'I love you, my son, and I bless you in the name of the Lord, the God of Abraham, Isaac, and Jacob.'" He did so, hugged my brother, and looked over at me. My father extended his hand toward me, and I reached down to embrace him. He put his hand on my head and started to cry as he said, "I love you, my daughter, and I bless you in the name of the Lord, the God of Abraham, Isaac, and Jacob." Then he looked at Clay and asked, "Did I do it right?" Clay nodded, and Dad's wife said, "You did good, Joffre, and now you need to rest." He died 3 weeks later.

Clay showed me how to recognize some of my own character defects while observing them in him. Because he grew and forgave his family for their limited parenting abilities, I learned to forgive others who didn't know what they did that offended or hurt me. We didn't ask to be born, and we didn't pick our parents. Clay told me that when he was young, he couldn't understand why God gave him the parents he had. He was not proud of the fact that his dad was a junk hauler before it was relabeled recycling. I reflected on wishing my dad were more like men at church. Trying to make sense of my dad's occupation and providing for his family left me bewildered and doubtful about men's ability to provide for me.

While being part of Clay's insurance business, I didn't have his expertise or ability to function as a partner or shareholder but I was the bookkeeper and I trusted him to bring home the bacon. (Since he was no longer observing Jewish custom, we did eat pork.) Clearly, in hindsight, my limited involvement left him at a severe disadvantage when he lost interest in selling insurance and subsequently lost his balance. When he no longer felt capable of juggling the books himself, he dropped them leaving me in a financial mess with Freddie Mac and Fanny Mae. The defaults spilled over on me ruining my credit.

So this man didn't turn out to be who he had portrayed himself to be—or was it who I wanted him to be? Did I portray myself as someone else? I admit, I seduced him. How else does an insecure, middle-aged, twice-divorced woman with three teenage children handle herself? How does a Jewish guy ostracized by his family, divorced from an alcoholic wife, and raising two children—one with special needs—run a self-employed insurance brokerage? After 7 years of marriage, I noticed a pattern.

He could barely go one year without trading in and purchasing a different car. The 7-year itch wasn't new for me but he had an unusual case mixed with seasonal affective disorder. Then I learned about the significance of the number 7 in scripture. It relates to spiritual perfection. It's part of God's creation and when He completed it, He rested on the seventh day. I contemplated Clay's relationships with cars. He wasn't happy with just one. His declining interest in work and obsession for cars seemed to be snowballing. It was as if he were in a personal relationship with his money and his cars and committing adultery with them in our marriage. I studied more about numbers and discovered the biblical year of Jubilee, when all debts are forgiven—a clean slate. In a Jubilee year, the crops are rotated, and even the soil gets to rest.

Maybe I needed a rest. I didn't feel particularly overworked like I did during the days of raising babies. There were so many days when I looked forward to their nap times so I could take care of myself, knowing they were safe in their beds. At this juncture I longed to tune out and turn off the outside stimuli. Rather than stopping the world and getting off, I wanted to drift into the clouds and dream of another place. I was too tired to read and too anxious for sleep to refresh my attitude and renew my strength. My husband's children lived with us and caused more interference than my children, who lived with their father. Clay's business was in disarray and out of sync with the IRS. I finished college, and all the children except one completed high school. Rest. That's what God intended on the seventh day. So if a day is as a thousand years, could this be a year to rest? It might help to rest for a year. I could do something different. But like waking up, when I finished my rest and returned to where I came from, I would still be myself.

I could have given up if I had anything left to give up. My mother died the year before my divorce from Clay was final. She never did meet anyone from a dating ad. At first, she liked my husband. He played guitar and was really into music like her and my brother. Then, over the years, she started to suspect he was up to something, before I ever put my finger on it. I made excuses for him when he had bypass surgery on my 50th birthday. Then, when he had issues with diabetes and weight gain, I made further concessions for his behaviors, chalking them up to stress over his health. It took another couple of years and uncharacteristic outbursts to diagnose his chemical imbalance and medication abuse. Faced with being on my own again, I scrambled to find a higher-paying teaching job before I was "age benched," but the flood of new teachers and the fact that I didn't have tenure overshadowed my experience. Thankfully, I did have a steady paraprofessional job in an elementary school and looked forward to refinancing the house. When the housing market crashed in 2008 and I received the foreclosure notice, l was profoundly devastated that my attempts at financial independence had been sabotaged by my husband's abuse of my credit.

I couldn't be mad at God, because I trusted Him to make right whatever I screwed up. But I couldn't make sense of staying in our circle of Christian Jewish friends. How could I say God was in something that seemed to go so wrong? How many people might lose their trust in God, hearing about the demise of our ministry and our marriage? We must have done something for the "kingdom to come" since the enemy of God was trying to destroy my hope. And, of course, there were those who had no idea of Clay's illnesses and those who only heard one side of the story. This was the beginning of my sabbatical. I needed a break from everything relating to churches and religions. It dawned on me that God was working on bigger stuff than me. It's not all about me but through me—whether I know it or not, regardless if I like it or not—that God communicates. It's not that I can't be satisfied in a marriage to one man. It's more likely that few men practice godly behaviors that satisfy a woman's need for the image of God.

Chapter 15: Dating In The Computer Age

And God said, *"Your problem, my dear daughter, is accepting authority from men. You need to trust me so you can trust them to trust me."*

C hildren's view of divorce is always much different than what we adults expect them to come away with. My third husband's two children lived with him when we met. For 14 years they thought of me as their stepmother, and after the divorce, it's like I died. I remember my daughter telling me after a holiday event I wasn't at, "I missed you, Mommy, and it seemed like when they talked about you, it was as if you had died." That made me sad, and I felt her pain and the pain of my own mother, because I was a child of divorce. I was struck by how often we hurt those we love just by being ourselves and living our lives for ourselves.

With each major change in my life, it was as if I were reborn. Every rebirth was a new beginning, a do-over, another chance to figure out what I needed to do differently. Like when I miss the perfect pool shot and re-create the ball placements, thinking I can do it better—and sometimes I do. Those are only practice shots, though, and they aren't that important. Eventually, the clock runs out. There is no makeup class. I can't redo the test or experience another Groundhog Day. It is what it is, and that's it.

All of these pieces of my life intertwined to bring me to the next level. It's as if my multiple marriages and divorces were rungs (not wrongs) on a ladder, each step up (or down) bringing me to a new level of learning. I'd been to the matrimonial altar three times and struck out of the relationships, not sure if I'd climbed higher or lower. I wanted to run away and join the circus. I could juggle, make costumes, travel with the carnival, and hide behind masks of comedy and tragedy. So, when I saw an ad in the local newspaper that a clown club met monthly in a church building a suburb away, I checked it out. In 2008 I participated in a Fourth of July parade as Sally Star in a red, white, and blue getup with blue stars painted around my eyes and a red heart painted on the tip of my nose. It felt like I was all dressed up and allowed to play in the dirt and with balloons. People wondered how I transformed from a Bible teacher to a clown making balloons.

Maybe I was hiding. I was waiting, and I was not running. Making sense of my choices and accepting the consequences knit together my knowledge and my actions and put me back in the presence of God. Who I had become was a result of where I'd been and the choices I'd made. My life was not a bad dream. I had some nightmares along the way, and some subconscious warning signs, but I freely chose the path I traveled. Everywhere I went God was there, so if I boast, it is for His glory. The point is, there is no point; everything is circular. All roads lead back to the Creator. "Okay, God. I give up. I quit trying to be part of a union like marriage. I can accept that I'm just not good at it."

I was working at an elementary school as a paraprofessional in an autism program and studying for a reading teacher's license, waiting for everything to fall into place or fall apart. I needed the license to get a higher-paying job in a school. The house mortgage was in its second extension from foreclosure, thanks to bailouts and Obama. Nothing seemed to be in my favor. My mother passed away from a brain aneurysm less than a year before. I broke my wrist roller skating and had to slow down for 6 months. I had no one to hang out with and no place I could afford to go. I had to do something. I was determined not to overeat or drink too much, and sex certainly was not an option.

Funny thing about sex: It is one of the few things in life you can think about that brings pleasure without actually acting on the impulse to engage in the act. The more you think about food, the more your body wants to acquire some and indulge. The alcoholic can hardly stop thinking about the next drink, driving him to imbibe. Smoking cigarettes or pot sets up a chain reaction for another hit. I spent most of my life denying myself, for fear of getting hooked. Afraid that my mother's phobias were visiting me, I decided to ask God specifically why I was alone, and if that were not the desire of my heart, when would He provide me with a man friend? After all, He blessed my mother with Gus, her second husband, when she was 40 and alone. Why couldn't I have a guy like the one who married dear old Mom? As I reflected on Gus's admirable qualities, I wondered if I had picked the wrong men. My friend Rose said, "You have a broken picker." Either God would fix my "picker" or He would have to pick a man for me. One way or the other, I decided I'd rather live in sin, accepting the consequences, than be married again, dependent on a man, and go through all the paperwork, changing my name and identity for him.

Maybe I could just get a date. I could meet someone at church, but that was doubtful. I wouldn't be going to any bars. And it was unlikely I'd get a date at the grocery store. People were looking for people through dating services like E-harmony. I decided I'd sign up after I passed my licensure test. Curiosity got the better of me, and out of boredom and loneliness, I searched Craigslist. What was wrong with me? Of course, I'd heard horror stories of meeting crazies on there. Truth is , there are bad, stupid people everywhere. I knew I had to be very careful, but I just wanted to have fun, Lord help me.

I failed the test and did not get my reading teacher's license. I'd have to find another $100 to retake the test the following month. It cost $150 to fill out the profile on E-harmony's Christian dating service. After I did it and got three possible dates, I wanted to puke. If I answered the questions on the profile totally honestly or according to what I thought I should say in my best light, how did these guys answer? They could turn out not to be who they portrayed themselves to be. At this juncture in my life, on a quest for fun, I knew I wanted to be on the back of a motorcycle. At least I knew what I wanted at that moment. All my long-term goals were washed up on some distant seashore, and I couldn't go back home. What did I have to lose?

I answered three ads on Craigslist from men with motorcycles. I met one for coffee, but he didn't bring his motorcycle—done. One guy used the wrong words to reply—an instant red flag for my spirit. The third guy agreed to meet me at a huge public park, with his motorcycle, and we'd take it from there. I had two more dates with Mr. Honda motorcycle man and then invited some friends and him to my house for dinner. He was an adjunct professor at a local college. I checked him out, so I trusted he'd be safe with my friends. That was a blessed event. But another side of Mr. Honda motorcycle man emerged. He took offense to some general comments about relationships and rode off, never to be heard from again. With all that, I contemplated placing my own ad.

WANTED: *One Good Man. God fearing, brave, and honest. Physically fit active sportsman. Prefer military veteran. Must have Harley-Davidson motorcycle.*

My closest friends, knowing what I'd been through in the past year, were merciless. I was open and honest about my situation and my plans to survive spring blues and summer heat. They thought they were well-meaning and righteous, but they came across as legalistic and judgmental. Convinced there was no Mr. Right, no Prince Charming, and that Superman had died, I wasn't going to let any grass grow under my feet. Making new friends and going on adventures was a chance I had to take. I believed God would watch out for me now, as He had done in the past. I didn't like the feeling of being set up and used, but God has a way of influencing others for Him and fighting off the enemy in spite of our limitations.

Separating the stages of my growth and getting here gracefully required four men. If I had to sum up my life using the men God sent me—or, should I say, judging by the men God used to get my attention—it might read like this.

1st Husband: Letters overseas vs. writing prayers to God.

2nd Husband: Letters of disease vs. healthy feelings and emotions.

3rd Husband: Letters from a disciple and bad poetry in motion.

4th Husband: Letters online - 'Til death do we part.

I never did post an ad on Craigslist, but I answered one more that said, "Looking for one good woman." We talked on the phone the Thursday before Memorial Day weekend. We met for lunch on Friday. I didn't know before meeting him what "chemistry" was all about, but I sure know now. When we realized we were responding to what the other was thinking, we both agreed that the person of our dreams and the answers to our prayers was here and from God. He didn't bring his motorcycle, but I had brought my riding attire in the trunk of my car. He offered to bring me to his motorcycle for a ride, so I copied the license plate number from his truck to my phone and sent it to my daughter, just in case. Feeling like a rebel with a cause—to live happily, in sin, if possible or necessary—I took a leap of faith and put all my cards on the table. Like John Legend's *All of Me*, they were showing hearts.

Chapter 16: Tell It Like It Is

It's been 50 years since my childhood in New Jersey ended and I took off to California. My choices got me to this point. There are no regrets, and I accept the consequences of my choices. The outcomes haven't always turned out as I'd hoped, but if I had not followed my dreams, I'd be nowhere. If I had made different decisions along the way, I would be dealing with different outcomes. It is what it is. I can't go back, and I don't know the future, so I live in the present. My 50th high school reunion is in August this year. They didn't know me then, and they won't know me now. The event is just one of those milestones in life that lets you know it's a matter of time before the last dance. It's my year of independence. It's a Jubilee year in which all past debts are cleared, and I get to pass Go and start another race, another game, a new life. It's as if I've been born again—again. I've been set free. I've found the missing piece, put the puzzle together, and found my voice, my passion.

If I learned anything in kindergarten, it isn't relevant now. What I learned from Mother is finally settling in. She unknowingly labeled me a delayed firecracker but could not have known all the repercussions of such a handle. By all standard measurements and tests, I was a healthy baby and developing normally, with a high IQ. My academic performance was rote and paced. Whether my emotional and spiritual development kept up with my age is debatable. Now it seems that time has sped up and then stood still. I think I'm younger than I am, but I actually think older than I feel. I feel empathy for the title character in The Curious Case of Benjamin Button, who was born old and lived in reverse. He spent years growing younger while everyone around him grew older and passed away. Before my mother was diagnosed with a aneurysm, we witnessed several regressive behaviors. We didn't recognize them as abnormal medical defects; she just seem uninhibited. She said what she thought and expressed what she felt. I think of her now and don't believe you have to have a "sickness" to be up front and outspoken. (Maybe the sickness keeps us in the background and quiet.) She taught me to say it like it is when I was tongue-tied in religious mumbo jumbo. It just took me a long time to put into practice what I was taught. What I've figured out is that I am not an obtuse blonde. I'm really, really smart in the knowing and just a little slow in the showing.

So all this self-analysis brings me to the end of myself and closer to the force, the source, the Creator, my God. I could be overcome with writer's block, worried that you, the reader, will think negatively of me. But then, how would you really know if I'm being honest or just using some sort of poetic license? Up to this point, everything I wrote was the truth. Everything I wrote came pouring out of me as I believed it to have happened. Then I rewrote, edited, elaborated, and exaggerated. In some situations, I've attempted to elevate the offended and excuse the offender. Bottom line? I've scored a point. I've discovered my passion. It was a spiritual journey through feminism and online dating.

I've been writing most of my life as if my life depended on it, only to confirm what I've known all along. All roads lead to the Creator.

"There, my dear daughter, you've always been.
Here you are, in your passion.
Pour it out, not as cheap wine or pearls among swine."

My search for the one true love of my life was a dream. What I thought I wanted and what I believed at the time was founded not on solid rock, but on shifting sand. I could worry about what people will think of me and risk losing my voice again, or I can bare my soul and get naked, as it were, in hopes that you will think more of God and where He is bringing you on your journey. I can sum up my road trips with my husbands, my matrimonial mistakes and divine retakes, in deeper, more passionate media terms of the 21st century:

1st Husband: By the book—Masters and Johnson, *Human Sexual Response*

2nd Husband: By magazines and the movies—Playboy and Linda Lovelace

3rd Husband: By the stories—Scheherazade and *Fantasy Island*

4th Husband: By the chemistry—the spontaneous reaction of individuals to each other, especially a mutual sense of attraction or understanding (*Wikipedia*).

I've decided that making sense of multiple marriages and divorces vastly challenges religion, psychology, and society. My spirit, mind, and body have been in a three-sided battle for 50 years. Thank God, I know who is winning. We live in an age where all of the original rules, the standards described in the Bible, have been discarded or rewritten. Since no one is capable of keeping all the rules, someone decided God's words needed to be edited. That's too bad for us humans. I press on to run the race with perseverance, knowing that change begins within and some things never change. There is a ripple effect on the ex-spouses. I don't know for sure, but here is my best guess as to their existence to date. Where are the husbands now?

1st Husband: Lives in the hills of California, riding a motorcycle. Retired after a steady career of 35 years. Wondering how the women in his life have contributed to where he is on his journey.

2nd Husband: Lives with his second wife in Minnesota. Worrying about people, places, and prices as a stay-at-home husband. Analyzing how his family can get along with each other and leave him alone.

3rd Husband: Lives in Florida, trying to stay cool and calm. Disguised as a car dealer, dabbling in obscure money markets. Warring with his inner child and all three of his wives' influences on him.

And God said, *"As for you, My Dear Daughter, I'm not done with you yet."*

Chapter 17: Where Am I Now?

I live in a small town north of the Twin Cities in Minnesota. Joe and I have been together 8 years. We got married 6 years ago, a simple ceremony here in the home that he owned on a 2.5-acre lot in the suburb of Zimmerman. Grateful and blessed is how I feel about our relationship. We established a fundamental foundation on a spiritual truth the first time we met. Both of us felt our lives were filled with ups and downs, travels and rebounds. After too many attempts at starting over and not acquiring the complete sense of accomplishment we had hoped to obtain, we were willing to let a higher power direct our steps. We were too old and too tired to pursue fame, fortune, or furniture. It was time to slow down, enjoy what it was that motivated us in our youth, bring pleasure to each other, and live every day to the fullest.

We've both spent nearly 43 years in multiple marriages. We wonder what it would have been like if we'd been married to each other the whole time. Instead, we continue to share information about our past lives, in other places, with other people. At first, there was an unspoken fear that one of us would slip and call the other by a former spouse's name. Sometimes, glimpses into the other's past stirs up correlating memories in the other, and we spend hours remembering where we've been and realizing where we've arrived. Some scars are obvious, and others are not.

Our life together meant new beginnings. Even though Joe was

born in Minnesota, he spent years traveling and working coast to coast. When he decided to stop chasing "the dream" and start living with the hunger to know more of God, he settled near the fishing and hunting areas he loved in Minnesota. There were few family members or friends left from his past.

Before we met, he was enjoying his young grandsons. At the same time, I was lamenting the fact that my grown children weren't married and that I had no grandchildren. I filled some of that void by sharing Joe's grandsons. Over time, we've filled our schedules fishing and hunting together. I learned the difference between a shotgun and a rifle and how to use both. Joe had to learn patience. Remember, I'm really, really smart, just a bit slow.

I'm still learning to accept authority from the man God put in my life. It's much easier when you know and believe God is working through your husband for your good and His (God's) glory. On the other hand, God is showing Joe how a good woman can be a spiritual teacher without actually leading or instructing. There is no perfect union here on earth, which means we've had our share of misunderstandings that lead to quarrels. It's part of life. Life is about knowing who you are in relation to the Creator. Life is about loving others and knowing that love is a choice. It's about communication and expectations centered around that truth and supporting each other on our God-given journeys.

I've had to let go of my expectations for an extended family. My grown children are just fine the way they are, as long as they know who is in control of the universe. They don't have to go to church for me to believe that God is working in their lives. After years of trying to avoid organized religion, my heartstrings were pulling at me for friends and fellowship. Maintaining my autonomy in marriage remains a thorn in my side that resembles co-dependency, and needing others to take my mind off me is a good thing. In hopes of both Joe and I making new friends, I prayed for a church. Not long after that prayer, Joe's daughter mentioned that she was attending a Bible study at Bethel Church in Princeton.

"Anybody can go to it," she said, "even you." Fortunately, I didn't have time to take offense, because I was immediately aware that God had answered my prayer.

The church did not have a pastor at the time I started going to the Bible study for women, called Coffee Break. Joe and I went to visit the church one Sunday morning after going out for breakfast. "What would you like to do after breakfast?" Joe asked. He was showing me his appreciation for helping him the day before. He had planned an ice-fishing trip with the grandsons and his son-in-law. In the morning, as he was getting ready to pick them up, his son-in-law decided not to go. Knowing that the boys would be disappointed if Grandpa cancelled, I offered to change my plans for the day and go with them. The boys were a handful, and patience and communication are not Grandpa's strong points, but we caught fish and had fun.

"I'd like to go to church," I responded.

"Church? Where? When? We're not dressed for church." Joe was surprised.

"Sure we are. It starts in 10 minutes. It's really close. We'll be just in time."

Somewhat reluctant but not intimidated, Joe took me to church. They had a special event, with the Teen and Adult Challenge Recovery Ministry singing. It was a memorable service because of the testimonies and the fact that I had worked for Teen Challenge back in 1999.

We continued to attend Sunday church services every week. I introduced Joe to some of the husbands of the women in the Bible study. Eventually, he found the other hunters and fishermen and some men who were part of a men's group at the church.

About a year later, Joe said, "I've got to tell you something. I'm really surprised about how my life has turned out. Not in my wildest dreams did I ever see myself going to church, let alone being part of a Bible study."

We made it to church nearly every Sunday, but membership was not ever on my mind. Being involved and having fellowship with believers was enough for me. Joe started hearing and reading about membership classes and asked me if I was interested in joining. "No," I told him. "I don't have to be a member to give my time or money to a church I already feel committed to." I had joined one other church in my life, because it was mandatory in order to represent organizations like Jews for Jesus.

Other than being a member of a professional clown club, my face and fingerprints were not recognized in any organization. Joe was a good sport as well as a great sportsman when I was in the clown club. He jumped in as a driver and put on a red nose occasionally. He'd brag about my being a clown, reluctant at first to admit he participated. But then, as people expressed fascination and joy in our efforts, he relaxed his stance. "My life hasn't always turned out the way I dreamed it would," Joe said to a church friend. "I envisioned myself growing up and being a member of a motorcycle club, not a member of a clown club."

In 2016 we did became members of the church. The season of clowning was over for us when the clown club disbursed in 2018. We have 120 acres of hunting land, and a shack to retreat to during the other seasons of our life together. We watch the sun rise and set in the woods planting food plots, blazing trails and cutting branches for shooting lanes. We had a pond dug so the wildlife has plenty of water. But the amazing volume of the babbling stream that runs between our two climbing deer stands is hard to describe. It's softer than the Atlantic Ocean, over 1800 miles away and louder than the ripples on our neighborhood local Catlin Lake. Maybe someday I'll have the words to write about it or the notes to record the melody.

CPSIA information can be obtained
at www.ICGtesting.com
Printed in the USA
BVHW042211140419
545514BV00013B/738/P